Become a greater translator with CGP!

The translation questions in Grade 9-1 GCSE French can seem daunting, but with this brilliant CGP Workbook, you'll be 100% ready for them.

It's bursting with exercises that build up gradually to exam-level translations — perfect for honing your skills. There's also plenty of practice on the key GCSE vocab and grammar you'll need to score top marks in the exams.

We've even included answers for every question, so you can be sure your translations are on the right track. It's like Noël has come early!

CGP — still the best! ☺

Our sole aim here at CGP is to produce the highest quality books — carefully written, immaculately presented and dangerously close to being funny.

Then we work our socks off to get them out to you
— at the cheapest possible prices.

Contents

Section 1 — Translation Tips

The Translation Tasks 1
Translating French into English 2
Translating English into French 4

Section 2 — Me, My Family and Friends

About Yourself 7
My Family 8
Describing People 9
Personalities 10
Pets 11
Style and Fashion 12
Relationships 13
Socialising with Friends and Family 14
Partnership 15
Mixed Practice 16

Section 3 — Technology, Free Time and Customs & Festivals

Technology 19
Social Media 20
Music 21
Cinema and TV 22
Hobbies and Role Models 23
Food 24
Eating Out 25
Sport 26
Customs and Festivals 28
Mixed Practice 30

Section 4 — Where You Live

Where You Live 33
The Home 34
Home Life 35
Shopping 36
Directions 38
Weather 39
Mixed Practice 40

Contents

Section 5 — Lifestyle and Social & Global Issues

Healthy Living 43
Unhealthy Living 44
Illnesses 45
Environmental Problems 46
Problems in Society 48
Contributing to Society 49
Global Events... 50
Mixed Practice... 51

Section 6 — Travel and Tourism

Where to Go... 54
Accommodation 55
Getting Ready 56
Getting There 57
What to Do... 58
Practical Stuff... 60
Mixed Practice... 61

Section 7 — Current & Future Study and Employment

School Life... 64
School Events... 66
Education Post-16 67
Languages for the Future... 68
Applying for Jobs 69
Career Choices and Ambitions.. 70
Mixed Practice... 71

Answers.. 74

Published by CGP

Editors:
Marc Barnard
Kathryn Kaiser
Louise McEvoy
Hannah Roscoe
Matt Topping

Contributors:
Laetitia Dimitriu
Sue Todd

With thanks to Jack Tooth, Christine Bodin and Rosamund Place for the proofreading.
With thanks to Ana Pungartnik for the copyright research.

ISBN: 978 1 78908 049 0
Printed by Elanders Ltd, Newcastle upon Tyne.
Clipart from Corel®

Based on the classic CGP style created by Richard Parsons.

Text, design, layout and original illustrations © Coordination Group Publications Ltd. (CGP) 2018
All rights reserved.

Photocopying this book is not permitted, even if you have a CLA licence.
Extra copies are available from CGP with next day delivery. • 0800 1712 712 • www.cgpbooks.co.uk

Section 1 — Translation Tips

The Translation Tasks

The translation tasks can seem daunting, but if you take them step-by-step, they'll look less scary. Read through the text and then tackle them sentence by sentence so that you can focus on each bit.

The translation tasks are split over two exams

1) You'll need to translate <u>two short passages</u> which will appear on different papers.

2) The <u>reading paper</u> will ask you to translate a short French passage <u>into English</u>.

3) In the <u>writing paper</u> you will have to translate a short English passage or set of sentences <u>into French</u>.

See p.2-3 for more on translating into English and p.4-6 for translating into French.

Keep an eye on the time

1) The translation is likely to be one of the <u>last questions</u> on both the reading and writing exams. In both cases, it's worth <u>quite a few marks</u>, so make sure you <u>plan wisely</u> and leave <u>plenty of time</u> for it.

2) Remember you can tackle the exam questions in <u>any order</u> you choose, so you could start with the translation if you're <u>worried</u> about it.

3) However, you might find it helpful to do the <u>other</u> reading and writing tasks first to <u>prepare</u> you for the translation and <u>remind</u> you of some of the words that you might need.

Derek didn't leave enough time to get to the exam, let alone check his translation.

Read the translation carefully before you start

1) In both papers, make sure you read the <u>whole translation</u> carefully before you start writing — it's important to understand the <u>overall meaning</u> of the passage before starting to translate it.

2) Make yourself some <u>notes</u> before you start translating. Underline words or phrases that look <u>tricky</u> and jot down how you might <u>tackle</u> them.

3) Translate by looking at <u>whole phrases</u> or <u>sentences</u>, rather than translating word-by-word. This will <u>avoid</u> any of the French word order being <u>carried</u> into the English and vice versa.

4) <u>Don't panic</u> if you don't know a word or phrase — use the <u>context</u> to help you work it out. Be <u>creative</u> and think of another way to express it — it's important that your version has a <u>similar meaning</u> though.

5) You don't need to write a perfect translation first time — you can do it <u>roughly</u> first, and then write it up properly. Make sure you <u>cross out</u> old drafts with a <u>neat line</u>.

6) When you've finished, have a <u>fresh look</u> at every sentence. Check your <u>verb tenses</u> and <u>word order</u>, and make sure you haven't <u>missed out</u> any words or sentences from the translation.

Tradu-perdu-ction — I bet this joke will be lost in translation...

It's really important to give yourself enough time to check over your answer once you've done your translation. Think about what your weak points are and keep them in mind when you're looking out for any silly mistakes.

Translating French into English

Translating into English is usually easier than into French, because you're more familiar with the sentence structure. You still need to make sure your English sounds as natural as possible though.

First read the whole text to get the gist

1) You should spot lots of words that you already know. This will give you an idea of what the text is about. Once you've got the gist, the context of the text can help you to work out any words that you're unsure of.

2) You can guess some French words that look or sound the same as English words, e.g. la célébration — *celebration*, la musique — *music*, le vocabulaire — *vocabulary*.

3) Be careful though — you might come across a 'false friend'. This is a French word that looks like an English word, but has a completely different meaning:

Alice suspected that Nicola might be a false friend.

sensible	*sensitive*	joli(e)	*pretty*	la journée	*day*	les affaires (f)	*things*
grand(e)	*big / tall*	le car	*coach*	le médecin	*doctor*	les baskets (f)	*trainers*
large	*wide*	la veste	*jacket*	le crayon	*pencil*	supporter	*to put up with*
mince	*slim*	la cave	*cellar*	le genre	*type / kind*	attendre	*to wait*

You'll have to change the word order in English

1) As you translate each sentence, you'll need to look carefully at the word order.

2) Adjectives often come after the noun in French sentences, but they usually come before it in English, so make sure they're in the right position when you've done your translation.

| J'ai mangé la poire **verte**. | I ate the pear **green**. ✗ | I ate the **green** pear. ✓ |

3) You'll also need to watch out for adverbs — in French these can often be in places that would sound unnatural in English. Make sure you read carefully through your English to make sure you've used the correct word order.

| Les filles aiment **beaucoup** la musique. | The girls like **a lot** the music. ✗ | The girls like the music **a lot**. ✓ |

You need to translate some proper nouns

1) You don't need to translate people's names, e.g. 'Jacques'.

2) You will need to translate any place names that are written differently in English, though. Here are some that could come up:

Proper nouns are nouns that refer to a specific person or place, e.g. 'John' or 'France'.

Londres	*London*	la Bretagne	*Brittany*	la Manche	*the English Channel*
Bruxelles	*Brussels*	la Normandie	*Normandy*	la Méditerranée	*the Mediterranean*
la Corse	*Corsica*	la Bourgogne	*Burgundy*	les Alpes (f)	*the Alps*

Section 1 — Translation Tips

Translating French into English

Tenses can be tricky

1) The exam translation will contain a variety of tenses, but you won't always be able to use the same tense in English when you translate the French verbs.

2) The perfect tense in French isn't always translated using the perfect tense in English. After you've translated a sentence in the perfect tense into English, re-read it and make sure it sounds like something you'd say in English — if it doesn't, use the simple past instead.

| Il m'a envoyé un texto hier. | *He has sent me a text yesterday.* ✗ | *He sent me a text yesterday.* ✓ |

3) There are also a few different ways of translating the imperfect tense into English — you'll have to work out which to use from the context. If it refers to a repeated action in the past, you can translate it using 'used to'.

J'**allais** au magasin tous les jours. → *I **used to** go to the shop every day.*

4) If the imperfect describes an action that 'was happening' in the past, you will need 'was' or 'were' in your translation.

Elle **faisait** du vélo ce matin. → *She **was riding** a bike this morning.*

Remember to check your answer

1) Once you've finished, reread your answer to make sure it all makes sense in English. It's important to leave time to do this, as there will almost always be some mistakes.

2) Some words and phrases can't be translated word-for-word, so you might need to change your original translation to make it sound natural.

| Mon frère a huit ans. | *My brother has eight years.* ✗ | *My brother is eight years old.* ✓ |

3) Keep an eye out for set phrases which you can't directly translate into English — they're quite common in French, so they could crop up in the exam.

| Paris me plaît. | *Paris pleases me.* ✗ | *I like Paris.* ✓ |

4) See if anything unusual stands out when reading it back in English. You might have translated a phrase one way, but it could sound out of place in the context of the passage as a whole.

5) Make sure you've translated everything from the original text — you don't need a word for every word in French, but you need to have expressed the meaning of the whole passage.

Sure make you don't your word order up mix...

Translating into English isn't so bad — at least you can speak the language. Just watch out for some of the things that don't translate very smoothly from French. When you've finished, make sure your translation still makes sense in English.

Section 1 — Translation Tips

Translating English into French

The most important thing when translating into French is to make sure you have translated the meaning of everything in the English text — even if French uses a different number of words.

Read through the whole passage first

1) When you first read the text, you might come across a phrase or sentence that you can't translate literally. If so, it might be because it's not expressed in the same way in French.

2) If this happens, think of the simplest way you know how to write the phrase or sentence in French — just make sure you've got across the meaning of the English passage.

3) For example, if you were asked to translate 'I cycle to work', there's no French verb for 'to cycle', so you would have to translate it as 'I go to work by bike' instead.

4) It's hard to know whether something sounds like 'natural' French, so just try to write as accurately as possible. Use the checklist on p.6 to pick up some of the most common errors.

Be careful translating verbs into French

1) Before you start translating, look at the English verbs and jot down the tenses you'll need to use to translate them into French.

2) Make sure you know which English verbs are translated using reflexive verbs in French. Underline any in the text so you don't forget the reflexive pronoun when translating.

| Laure feels sick today. | → | Laure *se* sent malade aujourd'hui. |
| We get up at 11:30. | → | Nous *nous* levons à 11h30. |

3) Some English expressions use a different verb in French. This is especially common with verbs expressing how you're feeling, for example:

to be hungry	avoir faim	to hurt	avoir mal
to be thirsty	avoir soif	to be sleepy	avoir sommeil
to be hot	avoir chaud	to want to	avoir envie
to be cold	avoir froid	to be right	avoir raison

Translation always made Gary feel a bit tense...

There's a lot to think about when translating adjectives

1) Adjectives need to agree with the noun they are describing in French. You'll need to think carefully about whether the noun is masculine or feminine, and whether it is being described in the singular or plural.

| the black skirt | → | la jupe *noire* | The women are tall. | → | Les femmes sont *grandes*. |

2) Remember to think about word order when translating adjectives. Some French adjectives change their meaning depending on whether they go before or after a noun.

| the former church | → | l'*ancienne* église | the old church | → | l'église *ancienne* |

Section 1 — Translation Tips

Translating English into French

You don't always need the same number of words

1) Sometimes there will be <u>fewer</u> words in French than in English. This often happens when you're translating the <u>present tense</u>.

> We **are going** to Italy. → Nous **allons** en Italie.

2) There are some <u>verb combinations</u> in English that only need a <u>single word</u> in French. Watch out for <u>expressions</u> such as 'to have to' (*devoir*) and 'to be able to' (*pouvoir*) — they don't always translate <u>word-for-word</u>.

> You **have to** listen to the teacher. → Tu **dois** écouter le prof.
>
> They **are able to** come tonight. → Ils **peuvent** venir ce soir.

3) Sometimes there are <u>more</u> words in French than in English. For example, most nouns need an <u>article</u> like 'the' or 'a' before them in French.

> France produces quality cheese. → **La** France produit **du** fromage de qualité.

4) Remember that French negatives usually need <u>two words</u>, even if there's only <u>one</u> in English.

> I ate **nothing** yesterday. → Je **n'ai rien** mangé hier.

Choose your words carefully

1) French sometimes uses different words for different situations, where the <u>same word</u> would be used in English. 'To know' is an example of this — use 'savoir' if you're talking about a <u>fact</u> or a <u>skill</u>, and 'connaître' if it's a <u>person</u> or a <u>place</u>.

> I **know** that he likes maths. → Je **sais** qu'il aime les maths.
>
> I **know** Georges well. → Je **connais** bien Georges.

2) Translating '<u>for</u>' with <u>times</u> can be tricky, as there are a few ways to do it. Use '<u>pendant</u>' for actions that have <u>already happened</u>, or <u>will happen</u> in the future, but aren't happening now.

> Amy worked in a café **for** a year. → Amy a travaillé dans un café **pendant** un an.

3) Use '<u>depuis</u>' for actions that <u>began in the past</u>, but are <u>still continuing</u> today.

> I've lived in London **for** five months. → J'habite à Londres **depuis** cinq mois.

4) '<u>Pour</u>' can be used with time, but only for things happening in the <u>future</u>.

> Soon, I'll go to China **for** a month. → Bientôt, j'irai en Chine **pour** un mois.

Translating English into French

Watch out for plurals

1) Make sure you pay attention to which English nouns are plural. Plural nouns in French will usually follow the articles 'les' or 'des' and have an 's' at the end.

> Sabine bought some beans. → Sabine a acheté **des** haricot**s**.

2) However, watch out for irregular plurals which don't have an 's' at the end.

> The animals were hungry. → **Les** anim**aux** avaient faim.

"You could've got us more than one, Sabine, I'm starving!"

3) Be careful that the verbs you use agree with the subject. If the subject is plural, make sure you use a plural form of the verb with it.

> The boys always played hockey. Les garçons **jouait** toujours au hockey. ✗   Les garçons **jouaient** toujours au hockey. ✓

4) Some nouns are plural in English, but singular in French. Make sure you learn nouns like 'stairs' (*l'escalier*), 'jeans' (*le jean*) and 'trousers' (*le pantalon*), and translate them correctly.

Check through your work thoroughly

1) Once you've done your French translation, go back through it and check that you've covered everything that was in the English. It's easy to miss out little words like 'very' or 'always'.

2) This checklist is a handy reminder of the kinds of things you should look out for when reading through your work. Learn these points and keep them in mind as you check your translation.

- Are all the verbs in the right tense?
  Demain, je **travaillais** dans le jardin. ✗   Demain, je **travaillerai** dans le jardin. ✓
- Are the verb endings correct?
  Tu n'**aime** pas les framboises. ✗   Tu n'**aimes** pas les framboises. ✓
- Do your adjectives agree with their nouns?
  La cuisine est **grand**. ✗   La cuisine est **grande**. ✓
- Are your adjectives in the right place?
  Il porte une **rose chemise**. ✗   Il porte une **chemise rose**. ✓
- Do your past participles agree after 'être'?
  Ils sont **parti**. ✗   Ils sont **partis**. ✓
- Is your spelling accurate? Have you missed out any accents?
  Ele ecoute de la **music** avec ma mere. ✗   **Elle** é**coute** de la **musique** avec ma m**è**re. ✓

Hâte-toi lentement — more haste, less speed...

You might feel under pressure in the exam, but it's really important that you don't rush — that's when you're bound to make silly mistakes. Leave time to check your work at the end and make sure you've translated every part of the text.

Section 1 — Translation Tips

Section 2 — Me, My Family and Friends

About Yourself

Q1 Translate these sentences into **English**. Before you start, circle the verb in each sentence. The first one has been done for you.

a) Je (viens) de Manchester.

b) Mes voisins sont d'origine suisse.

c) J'habite à Londres, dans le sud de l'Angleterre.

d) Mon cousin s'appelle Félix.

e) Êtes-vous britannique, monsieur?

f) Ta date de naissance est le sept août 1980.

How will you write this phrase? Translating it word-for-word won't sound natural in English.

"My name is Bob and I come from... Earth..."

Q2 Translate these statements into **French**.

a) My name is Yang.

b) My birthday is in November.

c) I'm seventeen years old.

d) He was born in Wales.

e) My mother is Belgian.

f) We've got a big house.

Think about whether you need to use 'être' or 'avoir' for each sentence.

This is an irregular adjective in French — it goes before the noun it's describing.

Q3 Translate these sentences into **English**. Before you start, write down the tense of the verbs in bold. The first tense has been done for you.

a) **Je suis né** à Glasgow, en Écosse. ⇒ ......**perfect**......

b) Quand j'**avais** six ans, j'habitais à Paris. ⇒ ....

c) Mes parents **habitaient** aux États-Unis. ⇒ ....

d) Nous **venons** d'Espagne. ⇒ ....

This sentence won't be in the perfect tense in English.

Q4 Traduis ce passage en **anglais**.

> Je m'appelle Priya et j'ai seize ans. Mon anniversaire est le quinze janvier. Je suis française et je viens de Paris, mais je suis venue en Grande-Bretagne il y a un an avec ma famille. <u>Nous habitons</u> à Londres depuis dix mois.

Think carefully about what tense you'll need to translate 'nous habitons' here.

Before you start, check:
- [ ] Tenses — have you identified the different tenses you'll need?
- [ ] Vocab — do you know how to translate the numbers in this passage accurately?

Section 2 — Me, My Family and Friends

My Family

Q1 Translate these sentences into **French**. Before you start, circle the subject pronoun in each sentence.

a) (I) have two sisters and a brother.

b) You live near your grandparents.

c) She is an only child. ← There's a specific phrase for this — don't use 'seul' here.

d) We live with my father and his girlfriend.

Patrick wasn't as furry as his siblings, but he was still a member of the family.

Q2 Translate these sentences into **English**. Before you start, underline all the possessive words. The first one has been done for you.

a) Notre neveu s'appelle Léo.

b) Voici mes cousins, qui s'appellent Jean-Luc et Daniel.

c) Il aime beaucoup son frère jumeau.

d) J'habite avec ma mère, mon beau-père et ma demi-sœur.

Q3 Complete the French sentences with the correct perfect tense form of the verb in brackets. The first one has been done for you. Then translate these sentences into **English**.

a) Ma sœur ......s'est mariée...... avec sa copine hier. **(se marier)**

b) Son père .... l'année dernière. **(mourir)**

c) Tes grands-parents .... en 1998. **(se séparer)**

d) Mon oncle et ma tante .... il y a trois ans. **(divorcer)**

Q4 Translate this diary entry into **French**. Look back at Q2 to help you translate this.

> Tomorrow it's my step-father's birthday. We are going to have dinner at an Italian restaurant in town. My older brother doesn't want to come, so he will stay at home to look after our sisters, who are twins.

Which verb is being made negative here?

Q5 Traduis ce passage en **anglais**.

> Nous vivons longtemps dans ma famille. Mon grand-père a quatre-vingt-douze ans, et il est toujours en bonne santé. Ma grand-mère est morte à l'âge de quatre-vingt-huit ans. Le secret de leur longue vie? Ils ne se disputaient jamais, même quand ils étaient jeunes.

When you've finished, check:

☐ Flow — does your translation sound natural in English?

☐ Pronouns — have you used the correct pronouns?

Section 2 — Me, My Family and Friends

Describing People

Q1 Translate these phrases into **French**. Before you start, underline all of the adjectives. The first two have been done for you.

a) He has straight brown hair.
b) She wears red glasses.
c) We have green eyes and wavy hair.
d) You have a long beard.
e) I have short blonde hair and blue eyes.
f) The girls are very tall.

Remember to make adjectives 'agree' with the thing they're describing.

Q2 Translate the comparisons in bold into **English**. The first comparison has been done for you. Then translate each sentence.

a) Je suis **plus petit que** mon frère. ➡ shorter than
b) Elle est **moins laide que** moi. ➡ ....
c) Maurice a **plus de cheveux que** Frédéric. ➡ ....
d) Il a **moins de boutons qu'**avant. ➡ ....
e) Ses cheveux sont **aussi courts que** les miens. ➡ ....
   The word for this in English is similar.

Q3 Translate these sentences into **English**. Before you start, circle all the intensifiers. The first one has been done for you.

a) Tes deux fils sont (très) grands pour leur âge.
b) J'ai su que tu parlais parce que ta voix est particulièrement forte.
c) Tous mes amis me disent que je parle trop vite, mais je ne suis pas d'accord.
d) Ma sœur aînée n'aime pas le fait qu'elle ressemble* vraiment à notre père.
   *ressembler à = to resemble / look like

Intensifiers are words like 'very' and 'really' — they emphasise the meaning of other words.

'Su' is the past participle of 'savoir'.

Q4 Translate this passage from an art magazine into **French**.

Do you think that the Mona Lisa* is beautiful? She has long brown hair, neither straight nor curly. In my opinion, she's less pretty than the models of today. But what's interesting is her air of mystery**. You want to know what she was imagining.

*Mona Lisa = la Joconde   **air of mystery = air mystérieux   Translate this using the verb 's'imaginer'.

When you've finished, check:
☐ Adjective agreements — do all your adjectives agree with the nouns they're describing?
☐ Tenses — are you confident you've used the correct ones?

Section 2 — Me, My Family and Friends

Personalities

Q1 Write down the gender (male, female, can't tell) of the speaker in each sentence. The first one has been done for you. Then translate the sentences into **English**.

a) Je suis sympa et bavarde, et parfois paresseuse aussi. ➡ ....**female**................

b) Normalement je suis drôle, mais je suis timide quelquefois. ➡ ....

c) Je suis assez égoïste, et un peu embêtant aussi. ➡ ....

d) <u>On dit que</u> je suis intelligente, parce que je travaille dur. ➡ ....
   ↖ How will you translate this? 'One says that' doesn't sound very natural in English.

Q2 Translate these sentences into **French**, thinking about plurals and adjective agreements.

a) We are very sporty.

b) Old people* are always chatty.
   *old people = les personnes âgées

c) Your uncles are never happy.

d) The girls are too noisy.

Q3 Write down the English meaning of the 'false friends' in bold. Then translate the sentences into **English**.

'False friends' are French words that sound like English words, but have a different meaning.

a) Elle a un **caractère** amusant. ➡ ....**personality**................

b) Mon meilleur ami <u>peut être</u> très **sensible**. ➡ ....

Be careful — 'peut être' and 'peut-être' mean different things.

c) Tu es vraiment **gentille** et ouverte. ➡ ....

d) Mon frère devrait être plus patient et **compréhensif**. ➡ ....

Q4 Translate this passage into **French**.   You will need the perfect tense of 'être' here.

> My mother is hard-working and generous. She <u>has always been</u> kind, and she has never been selfish. Even when I'm annoying, she isn't unfair. <u>Everybody</u> loves her.

Remember that 'everybody' uses the 'il' form of the verb.

Q5 Traduis ce passage en **anglais**.   Keep an eye out for 'false friends' in this passage.

> Quand j'étais petit, j'étais très réservé donc je n'avais pas beaucoup d'amis. En général, mes amis pensaient que j'étais trop sensible. Je suis encore assez timide, mais j'ai des copains maintenant qui sont plus comme moi. Ils sont beaucoup plus compréhensifs.

Section 2 — Me, My Family and Friends

Pets

Q1 Fill in the gaps with the correct imperfect tense form of the verb in brackets. The first one has been done for you. Then translate the sentences into **English**.

a) Vous ......**aviez**...... un animal domestique? **(avoir)**

b) Je .... des poissons tropicaux à chaque anniversaire. **(recevoir)**

c) Tom n'........................ pas les chevaux.   *This can mean 'always' or 'still'. Which one do you need here?*   **(aimer)**

d) Mon meilleur copain, c'........................ toujours mon chien! **(être)**

Q2 Translate these sentences into **French**. Before you start, underline all the adjectives that are irregular in French. There is one in each sentence.

a) Do you like all large animals?

b) My tortoise is very old and tired.

c) I have a white mouse called Trixie. She is very naughty!

d) I have two grey guinea pigs. They are beautiful.

The adjectives you need to underline use irregular endings to agree with the nouns they're describing.

Trevor couldn't remember where he'd left his dentures the night before.

Q3 The passage below has been translated from French into **English**. Fill in the gaps to complete the translation.

> Pendant mon enfance, nous n'avions pas d'animaux domestiques. Ma mère me disait que notre appartement était trop petit. En ce moment, nous avons un chat, mais si j'avais ma propre maison, j'aurais trois grands chiens.

When I was growing up, we didn't have .... My mother .... our flat was too small. .... , we have a cat, but if I had my own house, ... three big dogs.

Q4 Translate this notice about a lost cat into **French**.

Remember, when an object pronoun is used with a negative in the perfect tense, it goes between the 'ne' and the 'avoir' or 'être' bit of the verb.

> Have you seen our cat Marvin? <u>We haven't seen him</u> since last Friday. He is black and he has white paws*. I'm worried because he doesn't like being alone. We think he's in a garage or under a car. Phone us if you find him. <u>We miss him</u>!

a paw = une patte   *Translate this as 'he is missing to us'.*

When you've finished, check:
- [ ] Adjectives — do they agree with the nouns they're describing?
- [ ] Pronouns — have you included them all?

Section 2 — Me, My Family and Friends

Style and Fashion

Q1 Fill in the gaps with the correct present tense form of the irregular verb in brackets. Then translate the sentences into **English**. The first verb has been done for you.

a) Guillaume ......**veut**...... devenir styliste de mode à l'avenir. **(vouloir)**

b) Les mannequins célèbres .... à Londres en septembre. **(aller)**

c) Je .... ce qui est à la mode en ce moment. **(savoir)**

d) Est-ce que vous .... tous vos sacs à main en cuir? **(faire)**

Q2 Translate these sentences into **French**. Before you start, write down the correct perfect tense form of the verb in bold. The first one has been done for you.

a) Tight trousers **became** fashionable last year. ➡ ......**sont devenus**......

b) I **bought** some smart jeans yesterday. ➡ ....
 The noun for 'jeans' is singular in French.

c) The model **lost** his watch last night. ➡ ....

d) He **put on** his dressing gown at the party. ➡ ....
 The past participle of 'mettre' is irregular.

Q3 Circle the correct translation of 'which' in each sentence. Then translate each sentence into **English**.

a) Quel /(Quelle) est votre taille, monsieur?

b) Quels / Quelles genres de chaussures sont actuellement à la mode?

c) Quel / Quelle couleur de chapeau est ta préférée?

d) Quels / Quelles sont vos marques favorites?

Erin's satellite dish hat got a great reception.

Q4 Translate this diary extract into **English**.

Is this singular or plural?

Après m'être habillée, j'ai commencé à me maquiller. J'ai appliqué du <u>rouge à lèvres</u>, mais je ne pouvais pas choisir quels bijoux porter. D'habitude, je porte un t-shirt et <u>un jean</u> quand je sors. Cependant, j'ai décidé de porter une robe pour cette fête.

Look back at Q2 for a clue on how to translate this.

Before you start, check:
- Tenses — have you correctly identified them all? Pay careful attention to the first sentence.
- Vocab — do you know all the words you need for clothing and make-up?

Section 2 — Me, My Family and Friends

Relationships

Q1 Translate these sentences into **English**. Before you start, circle the two parts of the negative in each sentence. The first one has been done for you.

a) Mon grand-père (ne) m'aide (plus) à faire mes devoirs.

b) On dit que les adolescents ne respectent jamais leurs parents.

c) Tu n'as pas encore envoyé le cadeau à ton cousin.

d) Il n'y a personne dans ma famille avec qui j'ai de bons rapports.

This word is singular in English.
Translate this as 'with whom'.

Q2 Translate these sentences into **French**. Before you start, tick the sentences that will use reflexives in French.

a) My best friend Sara often argues with her sister.

b) Max gets on with his brother.

c) I don't really know my cousins.
Be careful — 'know' can't be translated as 'savoir' in this context.

d) Your brother doesn't speak to your step-father any more.

e) I like to go out with my friends.

f) My father and I get on well.
What pronoun should you use for a group that includes yourself?

Q3 Complete the sentences with the correct perfect tense form of the verbs in brackets. Then translate the sentences into **English**. The first verb has been done for you.

Remember that the past participle of a reflexive verb has to agree with its subject.

a) Elle ...... **s'est fâchée** ...... hier avec sa mère. **(se fâcher)**

b) Nous .... bien ensemble à la fête. **(s'amuser)**

c) Ma sœur .... sa nièce le week-end dernier. **(s'occuper de)**

d) Louis .... des amis facilement en vacances. **(se faire)**

Q4 Traduis ce passage en **français**.

Look back at Q1 for a clue on translating this.
Remember that when a reflexive is negative, the 'ne' goes before the reflexive pronoun.

I have a bad relationship with my sister. We don't get on well. She's always arguing with me, and she never listens to me. Our parents don't understand, because she's polite in front of them. Yesterday she stole my pocket money. I don't like her at all*!

*at all = du tout
Translate this as 'eux'.

When you've finished, check:

☐ Reflexives — have you made the right verbs reflexive?

☐ Negatives — have you translated them all? There should be four.

Section 2 — Me, My Family and Friends

Socialising with Friends and Family

Q1 Write down the French prepositions that you need to translate the words in bold. Then translate each sentence into **French**. The first preposition has been done for you.

a) Our parents like going **to** the swimming pool. ⇒ ....à........

b) My friends play football **in** town. ⇒ ....

c) Your sister is staying **at** Siobhan's house. ⇒ ....

d) He's coming back **from** Gethin's party. ⇒ ....

Q2 Translate the sentences into **English**. Before you start, underline the adverbs to do with time.

a) Tu fais de la natation avec Ali le lundi soir.

b) Mon meilleur ami me rend souvent visite.

c) Un nouveau café a ouvert près de la bibliothèque il y a deux mois.

d) Je parle tous les jours avec ma mère.

An adverb can be a single word or a phrase.

Q3 Translate these statements into **French**. Think carefully about how you will translate the start of each sentence.

a) Playing board games with my family is boring.

b) Going to the beach is a good way to spend time together.

c) Learning a new skill together has really improved our friendship.

d) Going cycling with my father is annoying. He goes too quickly. ← *Which verb do you need to translate 'going' here?*

Ten minutes into Family Games Night, things were a bit tense...

Q4 Translate this blog post into **English**. Before you start, make sure you can answer the questions.

> Je veux assister à un festival de musique avec deux copains, mais mon père ne me permet pas d'y aller. Je ne veux pas me disputer avec lui, mais ce n'est pas juste!

What does this 'y' refer to?   *Who is 'lui'?*

Q5 Translate this account into **French**.   *Look back at Q2 to help you translate this.*

> I met my best friend Solange twelve years ago. We are like sisters. We have the same interests, and I can talk to her about all my problems. Last year she came to Greece with my family and we hope to return there after our exams.

When you've finished, check:
☐ Pronouns — have you used the right ones?
☐ Tenses — have you used the correct tenses in each sentence?

Section 2 — Me, My Family and Friends

Partnership

Q1 Translate these sentences into **French**. The verbs in bold will need to be replaced with infinitives in French.

a) My cousin is going **to live** with her boyfriend after Christmas.

b) I want **to choose** my engagement ring. *The French word for 'engagement' is 'fiançailles'.*

c) My parents have decided **to separate** this year.

d) Nowadays the majority* of people are able to **get married** because marriage equality** exists in many countries.

*the majority = la majorité   **marriage equality = le mariage pour tous

Q2 Write down the correct proper future tense form of the verb in brackets. Then translate the sentences into **English**. The first verb has been done for you.

a) Mes noces ....**seront**........ très extravagantes.   (**être**)

b) J'espère que nous ne .... jamais.   (**se séparer**)

c) Tu l'................................ pour toujours.   (**adorer**)

d) Il .... l'homme de ses rêves.   (**épouser**)

e) Il est probable que ses parents ....   (**divorcer**)

Q3 Translate this opinion into **French**.

Translate this as 'pour plaire à'.

> Marriage isn't for everyone. Many people get married to please their parents. In my opinion, it's not necessary to marry to be happy. I would like to have children in the future, but at the moment I think my education is more important.

This comes straight after another verb. What form should it take?

Q4 Traduis ce message en **anglais**.

What does 'en' refer to here?

> Quelle nouvelle* fantastique, mon frère va se marier! J'en suis très content parce que je m'entends bien avec sa petite amie, ou plutôt, avec sa fiancée! Et je sais qu'ils sont vraiment amoureux**, donc je crois que le mariage durera. Ils habitent ensemble depuis six mois, et ils se marieront l'année prochaine.

*une nouvelle = news   **amoureux = in love

You'll need a different tense for this in English.

When you've finished, check:
- Flow — does the word order make sense in English?
- Tenses — are you confident you've used the correct ones?

Section 2 — Me, My Family and Friends

Mixed Practice

Q1 Translate these sentences into **English**.

a) Ma sœur est la personne qui me soutient le plus. Elle est toujours là pour moi.

b) Les filles embêtantes que tu as décrites, sont-elles tes cousines? Je ne les aime pas.

c) Nous avons huit petits-enfants qui nous rendront visite la semaine prochaine.

d) Ma tante Nora est presque toujours en colère. Nous ne nous entendons pas bien.

e) Théo ne parle pas à sa belle-mère depuis leur dispute il y a six mois. Je pense que c'est triste.

Q2 Translate this horoscope into **French**.

> This week, you will need patience* when you meet a friend. You will be very proud of a member of your family on Wednesday, who is stronger than you think. Don't forget the beautiful stranger** you met last week, because he has a gift for you.

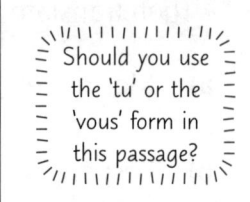

*patience = la patience
**a stranger = un étranger

Should you use the 'tu' or the 'vous' form in this passage?

This is an irregular adjective. How will you make it agree with the noun?

Q3 Translate these sentences into **English**.

a) Il vient de Belgique mais sa famille a émigré au pays de Galles quand il avait six ans.

b) A l'âge de dix ans, on m'appelait "Wiggy" parce que j'avais les cheveux très longs.

c) Je ne réponds jamais aux questions au sujet de mon âge. Selon moi, elles sont impolies.

d) Mes parents ont l'intention de déménager en Espagne quand je serai plus âgée.

Q4 Translate this relationship advice into **French**.

a) **Tanvir:** It's important to be open and honest with your husband or wife.
   Audrey: I agree. My husband is very understanding and he listens to me.

b) **Nkenna:** Try to get on with your partner's family.
   Fergal: Yes, I will try. I will ask my wife's sister for her opinion on the wedding.

c) **Freda:** Is it necessary to be your partner's best friend?
   Peter: Yes, my girlfriend never used to spend time with me, so we separated.

Section 2 — Me, My Family and Friends

Mixed Practice

Q5 Translate these sentences into **English**.

a) Même si on est une personne indépendante, pour être heureux il faut trouver des amis qui partagent vos intérêts et vos passe-temps.

b) Mes parents travaillent dur pendant la semaine, alors ils essayent de passer du temps ensemble en assistant à un cours de danse le samedi soir.

c) Pour fêter nos anniversaires, mes amis et moi dînons dans les restaurants.

d) Mes voisins participent aux activités charitables en famille pour aider ceux qui sont moins privilégiés qu'eux.

9 years later, Scott could still sweep Jo off her feet.

Q6 Translate this passage into **French**.

> When I visited my grandmother recently she showed me some photos of her wedding. She was very beautiful at the age of nineteen. She had blonde hair and green eyes. My grandfather was tall and strong, and she says he was the best husband in the world. They got married fifty-five years ago.

What tense do you need here?

Q7 Translate this passage about a historical figure into **English**.

> Marie-Antoinette était d'origine autrichienne mais elle est devenue reine de France au dix-huitième siècle. Elle vivait dans le luxe dans un grand château à Versailles, près de Paris, pendant que la plupart des* Français vivaient dans la pauvreté. Elle est morte le seize octobre 1793, mais elle est toujours bien connue aujourd'hui.

*la plupart de = most

Q8 Translate this conversation between friends into **French**.

Élodie: It must be difficult to have animals and a job as well.

Gérard: Yes. I have a dog, but my grandfather looks after him when I'm at work.

Élodie: I would really like to have a dog, but my step-mother's allergic to them. What would be your ideal pet, if you had the choice?

You'll need 'y' to translate this.

Gérard: I would like a horse, but I know it's impossible for me. Horses are too expensive!

Section 2 — Me, My Family and Friends

Mixed Practice

Q9 Translate these emails to penfriends into **French**.

a) My name is Ed and I'm eighteen. I have curly, chestnut brown hair and dark brown eyes. I'm intelligent and funny.

This word is invariable in French — it doesn't have to agree.

b) My name is Lucie. I'm shy with people I don't know well, but when you get to know me you will see that I'm friendly, patient and generous.

c) I'm Sophie. I used to be a very serious person. Now, I would say that I'm more sociable. My friends think I have a great sense of humour because I make them laugh.

Q10 Translate this argument between brothers into **English**.

Jérémy: Je ne porterai pas mon costume demain. Cela ne me va pas.

Sadiq: C'est le mariage de notre sœur! Tu devras porter quelque chose de chic!

Jérémy: Elle sera trop occupée pour se disputer avec moi au sujet de mes vêtements.

Sadiq: Si tu ne le portes pas, je t'ignorerai pendant toute la journée.

Jérémy: Ça serait vraiment injuste. Pourquoi tu ne peux pas me soutenir?

Q11 Translate these sentences into **French**.

a) My brother and my best friend are getting married this summer and I'm very happy for them. The wedding will be in Italy, because she is Italian.

b) People talk too much about love. I'm fed up with it, because it's the subject of every book I read and every film I watch.

c) Mehdi had a girlfriend last year, but they broke up. He has decided that he will never get married.

Q12 Traduis ce passage en **anglais**.

> Quand j'ai rencontré mon demi-frère, il avait déjà eu tout ce que j'avais voulu quand j'étais jeune. J'ai pensé qu'il était gâté. Malgré cela*, nous nous sommes toujours bien entendus. Nous sommes très différents en apparence. Par exemple, il est chauve**, et en comparaison, j'ai beaucoup de cheveux noirs et frisés.

*malgré cela = despite that
**chauve = bald

This word looks very similar in English.

Section 2 — Me, My Family and Friends

Section 3 — Technology, Free Time and Customs & Festivals

Technology

Q1 Translate these sentences into **English**. Before you start, underline all the conjugated verbs. The first one has been done for you.

a) Je <u>voudrais</u> un nouveau lecteur MP3.

b) Vous devez cliquer sur le lien pour voir l'article.

c) Il ne sait pas comment télécharger des images.

d) Est-ce que vous avez éteint l'ordinateur?

e) On ne doit pas s'asseoir trop près de l'écran.

"The download was meant to take 5 minutes, 40 minutes ago..."

Q2 Translate the words in bold into **French**. The first one has been done for you. Then translate the whole sentence.

a) **This** laptop was a gift from my cousin. ⇨ ......**cet**......

b) Switch on **that** DVD player. ⇨ ....

c) We found **that** new software really useful. ⇨ ....

d) **This** games console* is very expensive. ⇨ ....
   *a games console = une console de jeux

In these sentences, 'this' and 'that' are adjectives. Translate them using the correct form of 'ce'.

Q3 Translate these sentences into **French**, using 'est-ce que' to translate any questions.

a) Have you broken the printer? I need to print these photos for my brother.

b) I don't need these emails anymore. Can you delete them?

c) Can I type my message using the touch screen? I prefer it to the keyboard.

d) Did you send me a text? I didn't receive it.

Q4 Traduis le texte suivant en **anglais**.

The pronoun 'dont' means 'of which'.

> Je surfe tout le temps sur Internet. Cela m'aide beaucoup à faire mes devoirs parce que je peux trouver toutes les informations <u>dont</u> j'ai besoin. J'envoie aussi des courriers électroniques à ma correspondante*. J'utilisais mon ordinateur tablette pour accéder à Internet, mais il s'est arrêté de marcher il y a quatre jours.

*le correspondant = penfriend

When you've finished, check:

☐ Verbs — have you used the right 'person' of the verb?

☐ Flow — are you happy that the passage sounds natural in English?

Social Media

Q1 Translate these sentences into **English**. Before you start, circle all the adverbs to do with time. The first one has been done for you.

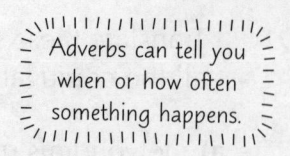

Adverbs can tell you when or how often something happens.

a) Claire utilise (toujours) les réseaux sociaux pour parler à sa tante.

b) John n'utilise jamais les forums parce qu'il pense qu'ils sont trop dangereux.

c) Récemment, il a commencé à partager plus d'<u>informations</u> sur Internet.

d) Il a déjà mis toutes les photos de ses vacances en ligne.

Will this be singular or plural in English?

Q2 The passage below has been translated from English into **French**. Fill in the gaps to complete the translation.

> I don't send messages on social networks because I'm scared of cyber bullying. Someone could pretend to be a friend and then start harassing you online.

Olivier preferred to send messages the old-fashioned way.

Je n'envoie pas .... sur les réseaux sociaux parce que

.... cyber harcèlement. Quelqu'un pourrait faire semblant

d' .... et puis commencer à te .... en ligne.

Q3 Translate these conversations into **English**.

Pay attention to all the object pronouns in this question. Make sure you know what each of them is referring to.

a) **Addie:** J'aime bien les réseaux sociaux. Je les ai utilisés pour tchatter avec Arnaud la semaine dernière.

   Darci: Moi aussi. As-tu vu la vidéo de sa fête d'anniversaire? Il l'a mise en ligne.

b) **Paige:** Il a écrit un blog sur le sport. Est-ce que tu l'as lu?

   Serge: Non, je devais créer un compte pour le lire, mais je ne savais pas comment le faire. <u>Tu peux</u> me montrer le blog?

You'll need to change the word order of this question when you translate it into English.

Q4 Translate this passage into **French**.

> I use social networks every day. They allow me to stay in contact with the family members that I don't see very often. However, my older brother says I should pay attention to what I share on social media. Last year, someone stole some information from his account and he <u>became</u> <u>a</u> victim of identity theft*.

*identity theft = le vol d'identité

Does this verb take 'avoir' or 'être' in the perfect tense?

You won't need an article here in French.

Section 3 — Technology, Free Time and Customs & Festivals

Music

Q1 Translate the phrases in bold into **English**. The first one has been done for you. Then translate each sentence.

a) **Ils jouent** du piano après l'école.
   .... **They play** ....

b) **Elle a joué** de la trompette au concert.
   ....

c) **Je jouais** de la guitare dans un groupe.
   ....

d) **Nous jouerons** du saxophone à la fête.
   ....

Q2 Translate these sentences into **French**. Before you start, think about how you should translate the words in bold.

In French, you 'listen something', so you don't need to translate the 'to'.

a) I know **some** gifted singers.

b) I like **every** song on this CD.

c) I listened to **some** songs on the radio.

d) **Each** morning, I play the clarinet.
   Look back at Q1 for a clue on how to say this in French.

Q3 Translate these sentences into **English**. Before you start, underline all the verbs in the imperfect tense. The first two have been done for you.

a) Quand j'<u>étais</u> à l'école primaire, j'<u>aimais</u> jouer de la flûte.

b) Leurs parents leur ont acheté un violon quand ils avaient dix ans.

c) Nous faisions partie d'un orchestre avant d'aller à l'université.

d) Il allait à tous les concerts, mais maintenant il n'a pas assez d'argent.

Q4 Translate this conversation into **French**.

a) **Lucille:** I've always loved rap music. I like to listen to it when I'm doing my homework.
   Nicolas: Me too. I bought a new rap album two days ago. It's great!

b) **Jérôme:** I used to be a fan of rock music, but now I find it really annoying.
   Agathe: I hate rock music too. It gets on my nerves. In my opinion, the <u>best</u> genre of music is disco because the songs are really lively.
   This is an irregular adjective in French.

Q5 Translate this passage into **English**.

This phrase is in the pluperfect tense, which describes events that 'had happened' in the past.

Le week-end dernier, je suis allée à un concert de musique classique. Avant d'y aller, je n'avais jamais écouté de musique classique. L'orchestre était incroyable et certains morceaux de musique* ont été chantés par une chorale formidable. J'ai beaucoup aimé ce concert, donc j'achèterai un billet pour <u>celui</u> de l'année prochaine.

*un morceau de musique = a piece of music

This is a demonstrative pronoun. Which noun is it replacing?

Section 3 — Technology, Free Time and Customs & Festivals

Cinema and TV

Q1 Translate these sentences into **English**. Before you start, circle all the infinitive verbs. The first one has been done for you.

a) Normalement, mes parents préfèrent (regarder) les actualités pendant le petit déjeuner.

b) Il va chercher un feuilleton avec une histoire plus intéressante.

c) Avant de trouver ce documentaire, <u>je ne regardais que</u> des dessins animés.
— How should you translate 'ne... que'?

Horace was horrified that his favourite TV show had been cancelled.

Q2 Translate the <u>underlined</u> phrases into **French**. The first one has been done for you. Then translate each sentence.

a) I like watching <u>romantic films</u> with my boyfriend. ➡ **films romantiques**

b) My uncle watched two <u>war films</u> on TV last night. ➡ ....

c) They told me that it is their favourite <u>detective film</u>. ➡ ....

d) She loves watching <u>animated films</u>. ➡ ....
— Translate this as 'films of animation'.

Q3 Fill in the gaps in these sentences with 'qui' or 'que'. The first one has been done for you. Then translate the sentences into **English**.

a) <u>Le film d'horreur</u> ...**que**... j'ai vu hier était très effrayant.

b) Je préfère <u>les publicités</u> .... me font rire.

c) <u>La chaîne de télé</u> .... j'aime <u>diffuse</u> des jeux télévisés.
— The verb 'diffuser' means 'to broadcast'.

d) Il est <u>l'acteur</u> .... joue le personnage principal.

Think carefully about whether the underlined words are the subject or the object of the verb. This will help you to decide whether to use 'qui' or 'que'.

Q4 Traduis le texte suivant en **français**.
Look back at Q1 for a clue on how to translate this.

> **Island of Ice** ★★☆☆☆
> After having watched the exciting trailer*, I went to the cinema to watch this action film with my sister. The special effects at the start were fantastic, but the <u>story</u> was too difficult to follow. I was very disappointed**.

*trailer = la bande-annonce   **disappointed = déçu(e)

When you've finished, check:
- [ ] Agreements — do the adjectives agree with the nouns they're describing?
- [ ] Past tenses — have you translated the passage using the correct past tenses?

Section 3 — Technology, Free Time and Customs & Festivals

Hobbies and Role Models

Q1 Fill in the gaps in these sentences with either 'donc' or 'comme'. The first one has been done for you. Then translate the sentences into **English**.

a) ......**Comme**...... elle adore l'art, elle peint chaque jour.

b) Ses cousins voulaient faire du ski, ... ils sont allés à la montagne.

c) Il ne lit que des livres .... il s'intéresse beaucoup à la lecture.

d) J'aime bien jouer aux jeux de société, ... mon père m'en a acheté.

Q2 Translate these sentences into **French**. Before you start, underline all the conjunctions and think about how to translate them into French. The first one has been done for you.

a) He will do athletics <u>if</u> you play rugby.

b) Even if it's difficult, I would like to practise fencing.

c) I decided to do archery since it seemed to be an exciting sport.

d) She used to have lots of interesting hobbies, but now she does nothing.

e) He inspires* me because he's a fantastic chess player.
   *to inspire someone = inspirer quelqu'un

Conjunctions are 'connecting words'. They usually link two different parts of a sentence together.

Q3 Translate this passage into **English**. Before you start, make sure you can answer the questions.

Which tense should you use to translate this first sentence?

> <u>Élodie collectionne les timbres depuis l'enfance</u>. Elle adore voyager, <u>donc</u> elle essaye de trouver des timbres qui représentent tous les pays qu'elle a visités. Il y a un an, elle a commencé à collectionner les pièces étrangères aussi.

How did you translate 'donc' in Q1?

Q4 Translate this passage into **French**.

Translate 'photographer' as 'photographe'.

> My role model is a famous <u>photographer</u> who takes photos of animals. I used to spend a lot of time at home, but he <u>inspired</u> me to go out in the open air with my camera. Usually, I take photographs of the countryside. I hope to meet him <u>one day</u>.

Translate this as 'encourager' here.

Translate this literally.

Section 3 — Technology, Free Time and Customs & Festivals

Food

Q1 Translate these sentences into **English**. Before you start, underline all the quantifiers. The first one has been done for you.

Quantifiers tell you how much of something there is.

a) Ils mangent <u>beaucoup de</u> fruits de mer.

b) J'essaye de ne pas manger trop de biscuits.

c) Il ajoute toujours un peu de sel à <u>ses repas</u>.

d) Elle ne mange pas assez de légumes.

e) Tu as ajouté trop de poivre.

f) Il y a peu de poisson dans ce potage.

↳ Is the word 'repas' singular or plural in this sentence?

Q2 Translate the phrases in bold into **French**. The first one has been done for you. Then translate the whole sentence.

a) **She doesn't like** cabbage. She thinks it's disgusting. ➡ Elle n'aime pas

b) **I love** salmon. If I could, I would eat fish every day! ➡ ....

c) **I like** Indian food **a lot** because it's spicy. ➡ ....

d) His mother <u>cooks</u> turkey often, but **he hates** it. ➡ ....
↳ Use the verb 'cuisiner' to translate this.

Q3 Translate this passage into **French**. Before you start, answer the questions below.

> My brother is very difficult. He refuses to* eat vegetables and <u>he only eats sweet fruits</u> like strawberries or pineapples. He also eats a lot of cakes and biscuits. <u>He will never eat well</u> and that worries me.

*to refuse to = refuser de

a) How will you translate 'he only eats'? ....

b) How will you translate 'sweet fruits'? ....

c) Which tense will you need for the underlined phrase near the end? ....

Q4 Translate this passage into **English**.

The word 'connu' is an adjective here, not a verb.

> Ma grand-mère a grandi* en Italie, <u>un pays bien connu</u> pour sa cuisine. Quand je lui rends visite, nous cuisinons des pâtes à l'ail et aux tomates. La semaine prochaine, c'est son anniversaire, et comme cadeau, je préparerai du poulet rôti à la sauce aux champignons. Mes parents vont faire un gâteau au chocolat.

*grandir = to grow up

Before you start, check:
☐ Prepositions — think carefully about how to translate all the 'à' + 'le' constructions.
☐ Subject — do you know the subject of each verb?

Section 3 — Technology, Free Time and Customs & Festivals

Eating Out

Q1 Complete the French sentences with the correct perfect tense form of the verb in brackets. The first one has been done for you. Then translate the sentences into **English**.

a) Tous les plats sur la carte ......**ont coûté**...... très cher. **(coûter)**

b) La serveuse lui .... une assiette sale. **(donner)**

c) Elle .... avant de finir son repas. **(partir)**

d) Le café n'était pas assez chaud quand on nous l'........................ . **(servir)**

Q2 Translate these conversations into **French**, using inversion to form each question. Make sure you translate the words in bold too.

Which 'you' should you use in these conversations? Think about how formal the situation is.

a) **Waitress:** Would you like to order a dessert, madam?
   Customer: Yes, I would like a slice of cake and the bill please.

b) **Customer:** I don't know what I want. Would you recommend this wine?
   Waiter: Do you want to taste it? I can bring you a bottle of it.

   The verb 'apporter' means 'to bring'.

Q3 Translate these comments about restaurants into **English**. Before you start, underline all the adjectives. The first one has been done for you.

a) J'aime aller dans les restaurants <u>chinois</u> parce qu'ils servent des repas que je ne sais pas cuisiner moi-même.

b) Mes parents sont allés à un restaurant de fruits de mer. Mon père l'a beaucoup aimé, mais ma mère a trouvé les plats trop salés.

c) Mes copains et moi, nous adorons les restaurants à tapas car nous pouvons partager les plats. C'est très pratique.

When I sea food, I eat it.

Q4 Traduis le texte suivant en **français**.

On Saturday, we went to a French restaurant. My friend ordered the soup as a starter. He thought it was very bitter. For my main course, I had ordered a well-done steak, but it wasn't hot enough. We <u>were still hungry</u> when our desserts arrived. <u>Fortunately</u>, they were perfect!

Translate this as 'still had hunger'.

Translate this using the word for 'happily'.

Section 3 — Technology, Free Time and Customs & Festivals

Sport

Q1 Translate these sentences into **French**.

Hint — the underlined words are all adverbs, not adjectives.

a) I swim <u>worse</u> when I'm tired.

b) She believes that she runs <u>the best</u>.

c) In my opinion, he played <u>badly</u>.

In French 'badly' and 'well' go before the verb.

d) He plays football <u>the worst</u>.

e) We know that we played <u>well</u>.

f) They will train <u>better</u> tomorrow.

Q2 Fill in the gaps in these sentences with the correct articles. Some gaps will also need to have a preposition. The first one has been done for you. Then translate the sentences into **English**.

a) Ils font ...**de l'**... escalade au centre sportif.

b) J'ai pratiqué .... voile quand j'étais en vacances.

c) Elle pratiquait .... badminton quand elle avait onze ans.

d) Je ferais .... natation si j'<u>avais</u> quelqu'un pour m'accompagner.

Think carefully about how to translate the imperfect verb in this sentence.

Q3 The passage below has been translated from English into **French**. Fill in the gaps to complete the translation.

> In the past, Polly was never interested in sport because she thought that it was a waste of time. However, after watching the horse riding at the Olympic Games, she decided to try it.

Polly found out the hard way that rollerblading and gymnastics don't mix...

...., Polly ne s'était jamais intéressée ....

parce qu'elle pensait que c'était une perte de temps. Pourtant, ...

regardé .... aux Jeux Olympiques, elle a décidé de l'essayer.

Q4 Translate the pronouns on the right to complete the sentences below. The first one has been done for you. Then translate the sentences into **English**.

a) Il pratique cinq sports et il doit s'entraîner dur pour ......**chacun**...... . **(each one)**

b) Je joue au volley avec .... qui habite près de chez moi. **(someone)**

c) Le joueur qui a marqué le but est meilleur que .... **(everybody)**

d) Il faut faire................................. pour soutenir les concurrents*. **(something)**

*un concurrent = a competitor

Section 3 — Technology, Free Time and Customs & Festivals

Q5 Fill in the gaps in these sentences with the correct conjugation of 's'entraîner' using the tenses in brackets. The first one has been done for you. Then translate the sentences into **English**.

a) En ce moment, elle ......**s'entraîne**...... deux fois par jour. **(present)**

b) L'année prochaine, les athlètes .... au terrain de sport. **(proper future)**

c) Je .... avec l'équipe scolaire le lundi. **(imperfect)**

d) Tu .... avec moi avant la course? **(conditional)**

e) Lance .... très dur avant le concours. **(pluperfect)**
   Is this a singular or plural noun?

Q6 Translate these sentences into **French**. Before you start, write down the negative forms you'll need to translate the underlined phrases. The first one has been done for you.

a) I don't play tennis because I find it boring. ➪ ......**ne...pas**......

b) They don't watch sport on TV anymore. ➪ ....

c) Our family has never liked athletics. ➪ ....

d) She does neither horse riding nor cycling. ➪ ....

Q7 Translate this passage into **English**.

Hint — this isn't talking about age.

> L'année dernière, je suis allée au Canada avec ma sœur pour regarder un concours de ski. Nous suivons ce sport depuis presque six ans. Le ski est plus passionnant à regarder que d'autres sports d'hiver. Quand je serai plus âgée, je voudrais apprendre à faire du ski.

Q8 Translate this passage into **French**.

Think carefully about word order in this phrase in French.

> My brother has been a professional basketball player since he was twenty. He has always been very gifted at sport. It was very annoying when we were little. Usually, I had to cheat* to win a game. I'm not very sporty now, but I like ice-skating at weekends.

*to cheat = tricher   Translate this as 'en'.   Which tense should you use to talk about something you used to do often in the past?

When you've finished, check:
☐ Verbs — have you used the right 'person' of the verb?
☐ Tenses — have you used the correct past tenses?

Section 3 — Technology, Free Time and Customs & Festivals

Customs and Festivals

Q1 Complete the French sentences with the immediate future tense form of the verb in brackets. The first one has been done for you. Then translate the sentences into **English**.

a) Vendredi prochain ....**va être**........ un jour férié. (être)

b) Nous .... la fête des rois. (célébrer)

c) Je .... aux défilés. (participer)

d) Elles .... tous les cadeaux. (emballer*)

*emballer = to wrap

The immediate future is formed by using the present tense of the verb 'aller' + an infinitive.

Q2 Translate these sentences into **French** using the 'on' form of the verb.

a) In my country, we open Christmas presents on the 25th of December.

b) In France, you celebrate Mother's Day on the last Sunday in May.

c) People wear fantastic costumes for Mardi Gras.

d) On May Day, people sell flowers in the streets.

e) People play music all day during the carnival*.

*carnival = le carnaval

'On' can be used to describe what people do in general. It can also be used to translate 'you' or 'we' when they refer to no-one in particular.

Q3 Translate these opinions about Easter into **English**.

a) Je pense que Pâques est chouette parce que la fête a lieu au printemps, et le printemps est la meilleure saison de l'année!

b) Pour moi, Pâques est une fête très religieuse. Je vais à l'église avec mes parents et puis nous rendons visite à la famille proche.

c) J'en ai marre de Pâques. La fête est devenue trop commerciale et <u>on a oublié</u> son vrai sens.

Look back at Q2 for a clue on how to translate this.

Flopsy was always full of eggs-itement at Easter.

Q4 Traduis le texte suivant en **français**.

Which pronoun will you need to translate this?

Last winter, I went to Switzerland for the New Year. I went <u>there</u> to <u>visit</u> my cousins who live in Geneva*. For them, the 31st of December is an important day, as people from that region celebrate a famous event in Geneva's history. We went to a special concert in the cathedral.

*Geneva = Genève

The verb 'visiter' can only be used with places. Which verb should you use to translate 'visit' here?

Section 3 — Technology, Free Time and Customs & Festivals

Q5 Translate this conversation into **English**. Before you start, circle all the question words. The first one has been done for you.

Question words are words like 'who' and 'what'.

a) **Gascon:** (Où) fêteras-tu l'Aïd el-Fitr cette année, Ibrahim?
   Ibrahim: Cette année, j'irai au Maroc où ma grand-mère habite.

This is a Muslim holiday that is celebrated at the end of Ramadan. Translate it as 'Eid al-Fitr'.

b) **Gascon:** Que feras-tu pour la célébrer?
   Ibrahim: Le matin, nous irons à la mosquée pour prier. Le soir, toute la famille mangera ensemble.

c) **Ibrahim:** Comment célèbres-tu Noël?
   Gascon: Ma mère est juive et elle ne le fête pas. Cependant, mon père est chrétien. Il veut que j'aille à la messe de minuit.

This is the subjunctive form of 'aller'.

Q6 Translate the phrases in bold into **French**. The first one has been done for you. Then translate each sentence.

a) All Saints' Day is **more** lively in Mexico **than** in France. ▷ ....plus...que..........

b) Our village festival is **less** popular **than** May Day. ▷ ....

c) For the first of April, French children try to put **as many** paper fish **as** possible on their friends' backs. ▷ ....

Translate 'backs' as 'le dos'.

d) Valentine's Day isn't **as** important **as** Bastille Day*. ▷ ....
*Bastille Day = la fête nationale

Q7 Translate this passage into **French**.

The verb 'dîner' means 'to have dinner'.

> A month ago, Louisa went to France to celebrate Christmas with her girlfriend, Camille. On Christmas Eve, they had dinner with her family, then they opened presents. This year, they want to celebrate it at their house. Louisa would like to make a Christmas cake.

What is this referring back to?

Q8 Traduis le texte suivant en **anglais**.

You don't need to translate this into English.

> Le vingt-et-un juin, c'est la Fête de la Musique dans toute la France. J'y suis allé avec mes copains il y a trois ans. Cette année, nous jouerons de la musique sur scène*. J'ai peur de chanter devant les spectateurs, mais je sais que ce sera une expérience incroyable.

*sur scène = on stage

Section 3 — Technology, Free Time and Customs & Festivals

Mixed Practice

Q1 Translate this advert into **English**.

> En juillet, nous vous invitons à un festival qui fêtera tous les genres de musique, y compris le jazz et l'opéra. Les concerts seront ouverts à tout le monde, donc n'hésitez pas à visiter notre site web pour acheter des billets. Si vous voulez plus d'informations, envoyez un e-mail à l'adresse suivante.

Q2 Translate this conversation between friends into **English**.

Fabien: Que prépares-tu pour le dîner ce soir, Simone?

Simone: Je voulais préparer du bœuf à la sauce au poivre, mais je n'ai pas de viande. Je vais devoir faire autre chose.

Fabien: Je vais à un restaurant italien. Tu pourrais m'accompagner.

Simone: C'est une idée formidable! Nous pouvons partager l'addition.

Q3 Translate these sentences into **French**. (EDEXCEL & EDUQAS)

a) After having left his job, my father started to look for new hobbies. He found a fishing club on the Internet. His old friend James is a member of the club too.

b) In her free time, Élodie likes playing video games. She recently bought a new games console. She can use it to record videos and share them with her friends.

c) Two years ago, I received an e-reader* for my birthday.
Before, I used to read actual books, but they weren't very practical.
*an e-reader = une liseuse électronique   ** actual = vrai

Q4 Translate these sentences into **French**.

The word for 'match' is the same in French. It's masculine.

a) My friend uploaded some photos from the hockey match.

b) Follow our blog to read all the sports news.

c) The footballers shared some videos of the best goals of the tournament.

d) She didn't watch the match, but her friend sent her the result.

e) I'm going to go on the Internet and look for the date of each race.

f) When I was chatting with Sadie on the Internet, she said that she couldn't come to the match.

Section 3 — Technology, Free Time and Customs & Festivals

Mixed Practice

Q5 Étienne and Aishah are having a night in. Translate their conversation into **English**.

Étienne: J'ai faim. Veux-tu commander quelque chose à manger? J'ai vu une publicité sur les médias sociaux pour une nouvelle pizzeria.

Aishah: Y a-t-il un menu que nous pouvons télécharger? Je voudrais savoir s'il y a des pizzas au poulet.

Étienne: Oui, je l'ai déjà téléchargé sur mon ordinateur tablette. Il y a pas mal de pizzas à la viande et les prix sont très raisonnables.

Q6 Traduis le texte suivant en **français**.

> Next Saturday, I will go to the cinema with my cousin to watch a horror film. The story takes place in a castle in the middle of a forest. My favourite singers wrote the music. My cousin hates them, but I am a fan of their songs. It will be great!

After seeing her grandfather in his swim-wear, Tiffany discovered the true meaning of horror.

Q7 Translate these sentences into **English**.

a) Il y a trois mois, ils sont allés à un marché de Noël en Normandie où ils ont acheté beaucoup d'aliments régionaux comme le fromage et les fruits de mer.

b) Ce que je préfère est le gâteau qu'on fait pour la fête des rois. Quand j'étais plus jeune, j'aidais ma mère à le faire avant la fête.

c) Pour la Hanoukka, on prépare les crêpes aux pommes de terre. Chez moi, tout le monde les adore. L'année dernière, ma sœur en <u>avait mangé</u> vingt avant le dîner!

Think carefully about which tense this is.

Q8 Translate this passage into **French**. *(EDEXCEL & EDUQAS)*

> Katrina's role model is an actor in a new film which will come out* next month. She loves watching his films because he is very gifted. She also respects him because he works harder than other actors. Her mother bought some tickets for the film online. They were quite expensive, but Katrina really wants to watch the film.

*to come out = sortir

Section 3 — Technology, Free Time and Customs & Festivals

Mixed Practice

Q9 Traduis les phrases suivantes en **anglais**.

a) Chaque année, il y a un festival de surf à Biarritz. Beaucoup de touristes viennent voir les surfeurs parce qu'ils sont très passionnants à regarder.

b) L'année dernière, je suis allé à un festival de sports extrêmes avec mon ami. Il en fait depuis plus de huit ans et il a participé au concours de skate.

c) L'hiver prochain, nous voyagerons au Québec pour aller au carnaval d'hiver. Il y aura beaucoup d'événements sportifs pendant le carnaval, y compris le canoë sur glace!

Q10 Translate these sentences into **French**.

You can't translate 'it' using 'il' in this sentence. What other words could you use?

a) In my favourite TV programme, a farmer shows us how to grow vegetables at home. It seems quite easy, but I think it would be difficult.

b) A few years ago, Neema took part in a contest on TV where she made dozens of little cakes.

c) An actress on TV has written a recipe book* to show that making healthy meals isn't as complicated as it seems.
*recipe book = un livre de recettes

Terry had finally found some dishes big enough to satisfy his TV appetite.

Q11 Translate Hannah's diary entry into **English**.

> Le week-end dernier, je suis allée au championnat du monde de badminton. J'étais assise assez loin du terrain, mais il y avait un grand écran qui m'a aidée à regarder le match. C'était très intéressant car les arbitres* ont pris des décisions pendant les matchs en utilisant les caméras dans le stade.

*l'arbitre (m) = umpire

Q12 Traduis le texte suivant en **français**.

What construction should you use to translate this into French?

> This afternoon, I went to a café that has just opened in the town centre. The owner is an actress from a children's TV show. When I was little, I used to watch it all the time. Unfortunately, the waiters were all very rude and the food was awful. I didn't leave a tip.

Section 3 — Technology, Free Time and Customs & Festivals

Where You Live

Q1 Translate these sentences into **English**. Before you start, circle the preposition in each sentence.

Make sure you don't get confused between 'au-dessous' and 'au-dessus' — they're opposites.

a) C'est un village (près de) Calais.

b) Nous habitons au bord de la mer.

c) La mairie est en face du pont.

d) Mon appartement est au-dessus de la piscine.

e) Son bureau est à côté de la boulangerie.

f) Ils habitent dans le même immeuble.

Q2 Translate the possessive adjectives in bold into **French**. Then translate the whole sentence. The first possessive adjective has been done for you.

a) Is there a big shopping centre in **your** area? ⇒ **ton** ....

b) There is a river between **our** houses. ⇒ ....

c) Yasmin lives behind **her** primary school. ⇒ ....

d) **My** town doesn't have a stadium. ⇒ ....

e) André doesn't like **his** neighbours. ⇒ ....

f) There are some trees in front of **their** block of flats. ⇒ ....

Possessive adjectives change to agree with the gender and number of their noun.

Q3 Translate this teenager's complaint into **French**.

Think carefully about where to put the 'ne' in this phrase.

> I don't like living in a seaside resort. In the summer, there are too many tourists*, so there's lots of traffic. In the winter, <u>there's nothing</u> to do. If there was more public transport, I <u>would</u> visit other places.

*a tourist = un touriste

What tense do you need to talk about things that 'would' happen?

Q4 Traduis ce passage en **anglais**.

> J'habite à la campagne depuis dix ans, mais je voudrais habiter en ville parce que c'est plus animé. C'est trop calme ici. <u>Dans ma ville idéale</u>, il y aurait beaucoup de bons magasins, un cinéma et un centre de loisirs. J'habiterais au centre-ville et j'irais partout à pied.

What does this phrase suggest about the tense of the verb in this sentence?

When you've finished, check:

☐ Tenses — have you used the right ones in each sentence?

☐ Flow — does the word order make sense in English?

The Home

Q1 Translate these sentences into **English**.

a) Nous habitons dans une belle maison individuelle.

b) J'habite dans une maison jumelée avec mon petit ami.

c) La famille de Gretel habite au deuxième étage.

d) Habitez-vous dans une HLM?

e) Nous avons un jardin très vert qui a beaucoup de jolies fleurs.

f) Fabien et Noémie habitaient dans une maison de taille moyenne dans une rue typique.

Granny's cottage gave a new meaning to 'home sweet home'.

Q2 The memory below has been translated from English into **French**. Fill in the gaps to complete the translation.

> When I was little, we used to live in a small flat, and I had to share a bedroom with my brother. Then we moved into a terraced house, where I had my own room. It was much better!

In French, describing things that used to happen needs a different past tense to describing a completed action.

Quand j'..................... petit, nous .... dans un

petit appartement, et je .... partager une chambre avec

mon frère. Puis nous .... dans une maison mitoyenne, où

j'..................... ma propre chambre. C'était beaucoup mieux!

Q3 Translate these sentences into **French**. Before you start, underline all the nouns that are feminine in French.

Remember that some adjectives like 'petit' go before the noun instead of after it.

a) In our flat there are three bathrooms and a small kitchen.

b) My perfect house would have lots of big windows in order to see the sun.

c) Your house is quite tidy, Henri, but I found a dirty dustbin in the cellar.

d) There's a problem with the oven and I need to make dinner. What a catastrophe*!

*a catastrophe = une catastrophe

Q4 Translate this extract from a magazine article into **English**.

> Si vous aviez beaucoup d'argent, quel type de maison achèteriez-vous? Beaucoup de gens riches n'achètent pas un beau château, mais ils préfèrent trouver une maison plus modeste. Souvent ils veulent l'améliorer eux-mêmes, en ajoutant* une piscine ou un gymnase au sous-sol, par exemple.

*ajouter = to add

Section 4 — Where You Live

Home Life

Q1 Translate these sentences into **English**. Before you start, underline the adverbs to do with time in each sentence. The first one has been done for you.

a) Je prends le petit déjeuner <u>à six heures et demie</u>.

b) Xavier fait parfois la cuisine.

c) Tu ne ranges jamais ta chambre!

d) Normalement, c'est ma sœur qui met la table.

e) Le vendredi soir, je nettoie la salle de bains.

f) Le week-end, mes parents font du jardinage.

Q2 Write down the tense of the verb in bold in each sentence. Then translate the whole sentence into **French**. The first tense has been done for you.

a) We **got up** at seven o'clock this morning. ➩ ......**perfect**......

b) I **wash** every day. ➩ ....

c) Vlad **goes to bed** quite late. ➩ ....

d) Émilie **used to wake up** early during the holidays. ➩ ....

e) When I was a child, I **got dressed*** very slowly. ➩ ....
*to get dressed = s'habiller

These are all reflexive verbs. They need a reflexive pronoun, no matter what tense they're in.

Q3 Translate these sentences about chores into **English**.

If 'poche' means pocket, what might 'argent de poche' mean?

a) **Marie:** Moi, je promène le chien pour gagner mon <u>argent de poche</u>. C'est génial!

b) **Julien:** Je lave les voitures de nos voisins s'il fait beau. Ce n'est pas trop difficile.

c) **Diana:** Je dois aider mon père à faire du bricolage le samedi matin. Je trouve ça fatigant.

d) **Akmal:** Je aime ça quand Amélie m'enseigne comment préparer les repas.

Q4 Translate this diary entry into **French**.

> Today was Mother's Day, so we got up early to make her breakfast in bed. While our mother slept, my brother bought some croissants and I prepared some coffee. Then we did all the chores* like we do every year, because she needs to relax.

*a chore = une tâche ménagère

Before you start, check:
- [ ] Time expressions — can you translate them all?
- [ ] Tenses — do they make sense alongside the expressions of time?

Section 4 — Where You Live

Shopping

Q1 Fill in the gaps with the correct demonstrative adjective (ce, cet, cette, ces). Then translate the whole sentence into **English**. The first adjective has been done for you.

a) Tu aimes ...**cette**... robe noire?

b) J'adore .... pantalon en coton.

c) .... chapeaux sont démodés.

d) Je voudrais essayer .... baskets.

e) Où as-tu acheté .... chemise?

f) Avez-vous .... jean en gris?

Q2 Translate these sentences into **English**.

Look at the first half of this word to work out its meaning.

a) Le jeudi, c'est le jour du marché.

b) La charcuterie vend la meilleure viande.

c) Moi, je vais à la boulangerie tous les matins pour acheter du pain.

d) Il y a une bonne poissonnerie en ville.

e) Tu as acheté ce gâteau à la pâtisserie?

f) Nous faisons les courses* au supermarché car c'est moins cher.

*faire les courses = to go / do the shopping

Q3 Translate these phrases into **French** using the correct partitive article (du, de l', de la, des).

a) Let's buy some coffee for tomorrow morning. I'd like a packet of biscuits too.

b) I don't have any salt, I'm sorry. But if you want pepper, I can help you.

c) I'm going to buy a kilo of potatoes for dinner. Do we have any garlic?

d) That slice of cake was delicious. Was there jam in the middle?

Q4 Translate these sentences into **French**.

Look back at Q1 for help on saying what something is made of.

a) He thinks that this coat is leather.

b) You have to buy a new pair of jeans.

c) How much is this silk scarf?

d) I like the woollen jumper in the shop window.

e) This jacket is dirty. I'm not going to buy it.

f) These shoes are too small. He needs size 40.

Q5 Translate these sentences about customer service into **English**.

What piece of paper do you need to have if you want a refund?

a) Je ne peux pas vous rembourser sans votre reçu, madame.

b) Le vendeur m'a remboursé à cause du dommage.

c) La ceinture était cassée, alors Louis s'est fait rembourser.

d) Si le client* dit qu'il veut se faire rembourser, il faut le faire.

*un client = a customer

This is an impersonal verb — even though it uses 'il', it's usually translated as 'you must' or 'we must'.

Section 4 — Where You Live

Q6 Translate the verb phrases in bold into **French**. Then translate each sentence. The first verb phrase has been done for you.

a) It **suits you**, Philippe. ⇨ ......te va......

b) That dress never **suited me**. ⇨ ....

c) Long skirts don't **suit her** at all. ⇨ ....

d) Does this swimming costume **suit me**? ⇨ ....

e) Those shoes **suit him**. ⇨ ....

The indirect object pronoun refers to who the clothing suits. Use the item of clothing to decide which form of 'aller' you need.

Q7 Translate this conversation from a market into **English**.

Translate 'marchand' as 'stallholder' in this question.

Christophe: Je veux deux cents grammes de champignons et un chou, s'il vous plaît.

Marchand: Voilà, monsieur.

Christophe: Donnez-moi plus de champignons.

Marchand: Ça suffit?

Christophe: Oui, il y en a assez maintenant. Ça fait combien?

Marchand: Trois euros quarante-neuf cents, monsieur.

In this sentence, 'en' is a pronoun. It's referring to the mushrooms.

There's no money in vegetable picking — the celery's too low.

Q8 Translate this cookbook introduction into **French**.

> I prefer to choose my fruit and vegetables myself at the market, where the food is fresh*. If they look good**, I will buy a lot of them. My parents used to take their time at shops like the butcher's, because you should always try to find good ingredients.

*fresh = fraîche   **to look good = avoir l'air bon

In French, when an adjective comes before a plural noun, 'des' usually changes to 'de'.

Q9 Traduis ce passage en **anglais**.

Look back at Q6 to help you translate this phrase.

> Ma copine Lili et moi, nous achetons souvent des vêtements ensemble. Elle sait très bien ce qui me va, et je lui offre des conseils sur ses achats* aussi. Récemment elle m'a persuadée d'acheter une robe jaune extravagante. Le week-end prochain, elle va m'aider à choisir une nouvelle tenue** dans les soldes.

*un achat = a purchase   **une tenue = an outfit

When you've finished, check:
- [ ] 'Aller' — have you translated all the different uses of it?
- [ ] Pronouns — have you translated them all?

Section 4 — Where You Live

Directions

Q1 Translate these sentences into **English**. Before you start, underline the imperatives in each sentence. The first imperative has been done for you.

a) <u>Prenez</u> la deuxième route à gauche.

b) Descendez la rue et puis tournez à droite.

c) Suivez les panneaux* pour l'église.

*un panneau = a sign

d) La gare? Tournez à votre droite.

e) Traverse la rivière.

f) Continue tout droit, jusqu'au coin.

Q2 Translate these directions into **French**. Use the context to work out which form of the imperative you should use.

You don't need to translate the roles of the speakers.

a) **Tourist:** How do I find the town hall?
   Mayor: Cross the bridge, then follow the signs.

b) **Child:** Excuse me, where is the police station?
   Adult: Come with me, it's not far. Let's cross the street.

c) **Actor:** Help me, please! I'm looking for the theatre.
   Busker: Turn left at the crossroads and it's next to the bank.

Q3 Translate these instructions into **French**. Before you start, answer the questions below.

> For your interview, come to our office in the centre of town. The entrance is situated opposite the building that <u>used to be</u> the post office. Go in and take the lift <u>up to</u> the third floor. Turn left and go to the end of the corridor.

a) From the context, which form of the imperative should you use? ....

b) What tense do you need to use when referring to the post office? ....

c) How will you translate 'up to'? ....

Q4 Traduis ce message en **anglais**.

> Il est facile de trouver ma maison, ne t'inquiète pas.
> À la gare routière, prends l'autobus numéro quatorze.
> Descends devant la bibliothèque, et tourne à gauche aux feux. Près de l'arbre <u>énorme</u>, tu verras une maison verte.
> Même si tu te perds en route, tu te débrouilleras. À bientôt!

This adjective looks very similar in English.

When you've finished, check:
- [ ] Prepositions — have you translated all their meanings?
- [ ] Imperatives — do the instructions all make sense?

Section 4 — Where You Live

Weather

Q1 Translate the verb phrases in bold into **French**. Then translate the whole sentence. The first one has been done for you.

a) **It's windy** in the south-east. ➡ ....Il y a du vent........

b) Étienne, look! **It's snowing**! ➡ ....

c) In Rouen **it rains** a lot. ➡ ....

d) **It's foggy** in Nantes. ➡ ....

e) Delphine says **it's cold** today. ➡ ....

"Levitation is snow laughing matter, Étienne."

Some weather expressions are impersonal — they always take 'il'.

Q2 Translate these comments about the weather into **English**. Before you start, circle the adjectives in each sentence. The first adjective has been done for you.

a) À Cannes, le temps sera (ensoleillé) pendant la fête du film.

b) Dans le nord, il y aura des nuages. Dans le sud, il y aura de fortes pluies.

c) Après un matin orageux, il y aura des éclaircies au bord de la mer.

d) Le ciel était couvert lundi dernier, comme d'habitude en Angleterre au mois de janvier.

e) La saison <u>pluvieuse</u> vient au Mexique, donc les touristes vont quitter le pays.

Use similar weather expressions that you know to work out what this word could mean.

Q3 Translate these potential plans into **French**.

a) If it's fine on Sunday, they'll play tennis.

b) If it rains this afternoon, I won't leave the house.

c) If it's hot at the weekend, we'll go to the beach.

d) If it snows tonight, school will not open tomorrow.

For this question, use 'si' and the present tense in the first half of each sentence, and the future tense in the second half.

Q4 Traduis ce passage en **français**.

Be careful — 'since' is a conjunction here, not a preposition.

> I would like to live in Spain one day, <u>since</u> it has a mild climate. I hate winter in this country. Last year it snowed every day for three weeks! <u>It will be</u> warmer in Spain than here. I like thunder and lightning when there's a storm, but I prefer the sun.

This expression is impersonal in French. The verb will take 'il'.

Before you start, check:
- [ ] Vocab — can you translate all of the weather expressions?
- [ ] Tenses — have you identified all of them?

Section 4 — Where You Live

Mixed Practice

Q1 Translate the following passage into **French**.

> Yesterday I tried to buy a new coat. I looked in all the department stores, but all the coats were too big. Then it rained while I was waiting for the bus. I was fed up! I'm going to try again tomorrow when I do the shopping at the supermarket.

Q2 Translate these details from an estate agent's website into **English**.

a) À Nancy, il y a un appartement chic avec deux chambres, à trois minutes à pied du centre-ville. On pourrait se détendre dans le jardin pendant l'été.

b) En février, on a vendu cette maison charmante, située dans la banlieue, tout près de l'église. Il y avait une grande chambre avec un balcon.

c) Cette chambre serait idéal pour un étudiant ou une personne célibataire. C'est une chambre meublée au centre-ville. Le chauffage n'est pas compris.

This is the adjective form of the noun 'les meubles'.

Q3 Translate this conversation between two friends doing some shopping into **French**.

Tibault: What do you think of this perfume? I think I will buy it.

Coralie: It would be an excellent present for your girlfriend.

Tibault: I agree*. Where do you want to go now?

Coralie: I was hoping to go to try on the jumper that we saw earlier.

Use the pluperfect tense to translate this verb into French.

Tibault: Good idea. It suited you well.

Coralie: I want to find a tie for my father too, and maybe some funny socks.

*to agree = être d'accord

Q4 Traduis ce courrier électronique en **anglais**.

> Salut Benoît! Nous sommes ici en Suisse depuis deux jours, dans la nouvelle maison de ma tante. Elle a une grande cheminée* au salon. C'est génial! Il a neigé pendant la nuit, donc ce matin toute la campagne ressemblait à une carte de Noël. S'il y a du soleil demain, nous irons au lac gelé.

*une cheminée = a fireplace

Section 4 — Where You Live

Mixed Practice

Q5 Translate this weather report into **English**.

This is what happens to cold things when they get warmed up.

> Enfin, le printemps est venu. La neige a fondu, le soleil est arrivé et il fait plus chaud sur la côte. Aujourd'hui serait une belle journée pour laver la voiture ou pour faire un grand nettoyage*. Il y aura encore un ciel couvert à Vichy, mais la semaine prochaine il fera beau partout.

*un grand nettoyage = a spring clean

Q6 Translate these directions into **French**. (AQA & EDEXCEL)

Translate each set of directions as if you were talking to a stranger.

a) The ice rink is quite far away. Take the first exit from the motorway, and then it's the second road on the right.

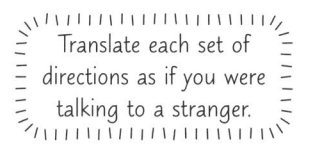

b) You're looking for the police station? Turn left at the lights and go straight on. After having crossed the square, you'll see it.

c) According to your map, you've already passed the railway station, but the map isn't right. It's over there, on the hill.

d) To get to the jeweller's, go down the road and cross the bridge. It's nearby. Could I show you it?

"It's no good, we'll never find the will to revise."

Q7 Translate these sentences about Annaliese's ideal home into **English**.

a) J'ai toujours rêvé d'une maison individuelle, loin du centre-ville, parce que mes parents habitaient à la campagne.

b) Il faut que la maison ait au moins quatre chambres, deux salles de bains et beaucoup de fenêtres.

c) Je voudrais aussi habiter près d'un arrêt de bus pour aller facilement en ville et faire des achats avec mes copines.

d) Je veux habiter à l'étranger un jour, où je pourrais avoir ma propre piscine en plein air. Il faut que je devienne très riche!

Q8 Traduis ce passage en **français**. (AQA & EDEXCEL)

> I'm fed up with my son. At weekends he sleeps until midday and then goes to bed really late. He never helps me clean the house, and yesterday he left dirty plates all over the kitchen. I won't miss him when he moves out next year!

Translate this as 'he will not be missing to me'.

Section 4 — Where You Live

Mixed Practice

Q9 Translate this newspaper ad into **English**.

> Situé derrière la mairie, le nouveau marché a ouvert samedi. Il vend des spécialités régionales et des produits internationaux à des prix très raisonnables. Voudriez-vous essayer notre nourriture? Ce dimanche, chaque client recevra un sac gratuit de cerises, et il y aura 30% de réduction sur nos boîtes de pâté de canard cette semaine!

Dennis had a bad feeling about this week...

Q10 Traduis ce dialogue en **francais**.

Lena: I'm sorry, but I'm going to be late. I had an argument with my mother.

Paul: Why did you argue?

Lena: I couldn't find my purse, so she made me tidy my room before going out.

Paul: That's unfair!

Lena: Exactly! I'm really angry, and now there's a traffic jam! Meet me at 11 o'clock.

Paul: Of course. I'll wait for you in front of the museum.

Q11 Translate these statements about Luc's search for a new house into **French**.

a) We must have a big garden because I love looking at flowers on sunny afternoons. Having two gardens would be ideal. One behind the house and the other in front of it.

b) In my opinion, the most important thing is a big kitchen, where you can make delicious hot meals when it's cold outside.

c) If we had a beautiful bedroom with lots of wardrobes for my partner's clothes, that would be perfect. In our former house, there were clothes everywhere!

Q12 Translate this shop notice into **English**.

> Vérifiez vos achats à la caisse avant de quitter le magasin, et gardez le reçu. Si vous découvrez un problème avec vos vêtements, il faut que vous nous le disiez pour que* nous puissions vous rembourser. Plus tard, si vous décidez que vous n'aimez pas les produits, nous ne vous offrirons qu'un échange.

*pour que = so that

Section 4 — Where You Live

Section 5 — Lifestyle and Social & Global Issues

Healthy Living

Q1 Rewrite the adjectives in brackets as adverbs on the lines below. The first one has been done for you. Then translate the sentences into **English**.

a) Mes parents préfèrent ......**vraiment**...... marcher. **(vrai)**

b) Didier fait de l'exercice .... **(rare)**

c) Je mangerai .... plus de fruits à l'avenir. **(certain)**

d) Au lycée, on nous enseigne à manger .... **(sain)**
   Translate this sentence into the passive in English.
   The word 'sain' means 'healthy'.

Q2 Translate the sentences below into **French**. Before you start, think about how you should translate the present participles in bold.

a) Gabriel relaxes by **doing** yoga each morning.
   This is the same word in French, and it's masculine.

b) Julie trains every week while **listening** to music.

c) We talk to each other while **walking** in the park.

d) By **eating** balanced* meals, Sandrine will stay in good health.
   *balanced = équilibré

To form the present participle, get the imperfect stem of the verb and add '-ant'. Use 'en' to translate 'by' and 'while'.

Q3 Traduis ce passage en **anglais**.

You will need more words for these in English than in French.

> Je n'ai jamais fait de régime. À mon avis, il faut manger équilibré. Mes parents et moi mangeons beaucoup de légumes. Pourtant, je grignote* souvent entre les repas. Je sais que c'est mauvais pour la santé, donc j'ai décidé que je renoncerai** complètement aux bonbons.

*grignoter = to snack   **renoncer à = to give up   *You can't translate this as 'the' in English.*

Q4 Translate this passage into **French**.

Remember that 'in' is translated as 'au' before the French word for spring.

> I only eat healthy food and I do lots of exercise. At the moment, I'm training for the Paris Marathon*, which I will do in spring. I have started to run every day. Now I have more energy, I sleep better and I am rarely ill. I will continue to run in the future.

*Paris Marathon = le marathon de Paris

When you've finished, check:

☐ Comparatives — have you translated them all accurately?

☐ Adverbs — have you translated these correctly? Think carefully about where each one should go.

Unhealthy Living

Q1 Complete the French sentences below using the superlative 'the most' and the adjectives in brackets. The first one has been done for you. Then translate the sentences into **English**.

a) À mon avis, l'alcool est la drogue ...la plus dangereuse.... . **(dangereux)**

b) Je ne fume plus parce que le tabac a l'odeur .... **(dégoûtant)**

c) Natalie croit qu'arrêter de fumer est la chose .... **(difficile)**

d) Sans doute, le tabagisme et les drogues sont .... **(nocif*)**
   *nocif — harmful

Q2 Translate the sentences below into **French**.

In 'si' clauses, the conditional is always used with the imperfect tense.

a) If she drank alcohol, Camille would feel ill.

b) I would feel better if I ate more fruit and vegetables. — *These words are plural in French.*

c) You could become addicted if you took medication frequently.

d) If Hassan took drugs, I wouldn't want to be his friend any more.
   — *Translate this using a reflexive verb.*

My mum told me to eat more fruit, so I helped myself to another slice of apple pie.

Q3 The passage below has been translated from English into **French**. Fill in the gaps to complete the translation.

> Roger believes that it would be really difficult to eat healthily if he didn't live at his parents' house. Unhealthy food is a lot less expensive and he only likes eating fast food.

Roger croit qu'il .... vraiment difficile de manger sainement s'il

.... chez ses parents. La nourriture malsaine est

.... et il .... du fast-food.

Q4 Translate this passage into **English**.

> Mon meilleur ami a commencé à fumer du cannabis. Ça m'inquiète parce que le cannabis peut causer des problèmes de santé mentale. Moi, je ne l'essayerais jamais parce que c'est trop nocif. Qu'est-ce que je devrais faire ? Je voudrais dire à quelqu'un qu'il en fume, mais je ne veux pas perdre un ami.

When you've finished, check:
- Tenses — are all the verbs in the correct tense?
- Flow — does it sound like something you'd say in English?

Section 5 — Lifestyle and Social & Global Issues

Illnesses

Q1 Translate the sentences below into **French**.

Use 'avoir mal' with 'au', 'à l'', 'à la' or 'aux' to say that something is hurting.

a) I've eaten too much, so I have stomach ache.

b) If you drink too many sugary drinks, Nina, you will have toothache.

c) They've had a sore throat for a week. — *Be careful — you can't use 'parce que' here because it can only be used before a verb.*

d) Delphine has sore feet <u>because of</u> her new shoes.

Q2 Translate the phrases in bold using the correct form of 'se casser' and 'se faire mal'. Then translate the sentences into **French**.

When you're talking in the perfect tense about breaking or hurting a specific body part, 'se casser' and 'se faire mal' act differently — they don't agree with their subject.

a) **Coralie broke her arm** when she was younger. ➡ **Coralie s'est cassé le bras**

b) **I hurt my foot** while playing football. ➡ ....

c) **They broke their legs** in front of the hospital. ➡ ....

d) **Hugo injured his back** when he had an <u>accident</u>. ➡ ....
   This is the same in French. Look at the ending to work out whether it's masculine or feminine.

Q3 Translate these conversations into **English**.

Remember to translate the word 'médecin' too.

a) **Thomas:** Je ne peux pas m'arrêter de tousser. Ce matin j'étais essoufflé et je me sentais faible.

   Médecin: Ce n'est sans doute qu'<u>un rhume</u>. Prenez ce sirop tous les soirs avant de dormir et vous vous sentirez bientôt mieux. ← *Translate 'un rhume' as 'a cold'.*

b) **Caroline:** Je ne me sens pas bien. J'ai de la fièvre et j'ai vomi trois fois aujourd'hui.

   Médecin: Il me semble que vous avez la grippe*. Vous devriez <u>rester</u> au lit jusqu'à ce que vous ne vous sentiez plus malade.
   la grippe = the flu

   Be careful — this is a false friend.

Q4 Traduis ce passage en **français**.

Use 'en' with the present participle of 'faire' to translate this.

> My brother hurt himself <u>while riding</u> his bike. We went to the hospital by car. His arm was very red and he told us that the pain was unbearable*. The doctor saw his arm and he said that my brother <u>had broken it</u>. When we got home, he went to bed immediately.

unbearable = insupportable

Translate this pluperfect using a reflexive verb. The word for 'it' will go after the reflexive pronoun.

Before you start, check:
- [ ] Reflexives — do you know which verbs will be reflexive in French?
- [ ] Past tenses — do you know where you need to use the pluperfect, imperfect and perfect tenses?

Section 5 — Lifestyle and Social & Global Issues

Environmental Problems

Q1 Translate these sentences into **English**. Think carefully about how to translate all the proper future tense verbs in bold.

a) Il y **aura** de plus en plus d'ordures dans la mer à l'avenir.

b) Notre quartier **deviendra** plus sale si nous laissons des ordures partout.

c) Le monde **sera** trop pollué si on continue à utiliser des sacs en plastique.

d) Les entreprises **devront** utiliser moins d'emballage* pour leurs produits.
*l'emballage = packaging

Q2 Translate these sentences about natural disasters into **French**.

a) Natural catastrophes like earthquakes are terrible.

b) Climate change* has caused floods in certain regions.
*climate change = le changement climatique

c) There are often forest fires in hot countries. ← Translate 'forest fires' into French as 'fires of forest'.

d) Droughts** rarely take place in this country.
**drought = la sécheresse

Q3 Complete the sentences below using the correct pluperfect tense form of each verb in brackets. The first one has been done for you. Then translate the sentences into **English**.

a) Carole ......**avait compris**...... les désavantages de l'énergie nucléaire. **(comprendre)**

b) Frédéric et Amélie .... trop d'ordures à la maison. **(produire)**

c) Henri m'............................ des dangers du changement climatique. **(avertir)**

d) J' .... le recyclage avant la réunion. **(trier*)**
*trier = to sort out

Q4 Translate this passage into **French**. Before you start, answer the questions below.

> In my opinion, we don't do enough to stop global warming. One of the most serious problems today is deforestation*. We destroy forests every year. We should protect them, but the problem is complicated.

*deforestation = le déboisement

a) What subject pronoun will you use to translate 'we' into French? ....

b) How will you translate 'enough' into French? ....

c) What verb will you use to translate 'we should'? ....

Section 5 — Lifestyle and Social & Global Issues

Q5 Complete the sentences below using the comparative or superlative in brackets. The first one has been done for you. Then translate the sentences into **English**.

The missing words are all adjectives, so they'll need to agree with what they're describing.

a) La qualité de l'eau de la rivière est devenue ……**meilleure**…… récemment. **(better)**

b) Notre ville a …………………… niveaux de pollution de l'air dans la région. **(the worst)**

c) Les forêts sont …………………… chose pour rendre l'air plus propre. **(the best)**

d) Le problème du <u>pétrole</u> dans la mer devient …………………… . **(worse)**

Watch out — this doesn't mean 'petrol'. What else could it be?

Q6 Traduis ce passage en **français**.

I am very angry because of the rubbish in our area. We used to live in a beautiful village with lots of green spaces, but now our <u>environment</u> is damaged. Soon it will be too late. We must change our behaviour* and look after the countryside.

*behaviour = le comportement

This is spelt slightly differently in French.

Q7 Translate these opinions on energy into **French**.

Translate 'to' using 'à' and a definite article.

a) **Alain:** New types of energy will be the only solution <u>to</u> global warming.

b) **Fleur:** Renewable energy will not be able to produce enough electricity.

c) **Alex:** We used to use a lot of coal to create electricity, but it was <u>bad</u> for the environment.

The word 'mauvais' is an adjective and 'mal' is an adverb. Which do you need to translate 'bad' here?

d) **Ida:** There's too much pollution in the air. We should stop burning* oil.

*to burn = brûler

Robert was finding his new renewable electricity generator quite exhausting.

Q8 Translate this passage into **English**.

Ma famille et moi faisons un grand effort pour <u>protéger</u> l'environnement. Mes parents ont vendu leur voiture et ils vont au travail à pied. S'il y avait des <u>pistes cyclables</u> dans ma ville, mes parents iraient partout en vélo. Nous croyons qu'il est important de réduire le <u>gaz carbonique</u> dans l'atmosphère.

Before you start, check:
- [ ] Vocab — can you translate all of the underlined words?
- [ ] Tenses — there are four tenses in the text. Do you know how to translate them all?

Section 5 — Lifestyle and Social & Global Issues

Problems in Society

Q1 Read the sentences below and put a tick next to the underlined nouns that will need a definite article (le, la, l' or les) in French. Then translate each sentence into **French**.

a) <u>Poverty</u> ☐ is a very serious problem in society.

b) There is a lot of <u>unemployment</u> ☐ in my town.

c) There isn't enough <u>drinking water</u> ☐.

d) <u>Bullying</u> ☐ takes place at schools and at work.

e) It seems to me that the <u>problem</u> ☐ of racism is becoming worse.

When a noun comes straight after an expression of quantity in French, it usually doesn't need a definite article.

Q2 Translate the impersonal constructions in bold below into **French**. Then translate the rest of each sentence.

Translate these impersonal constructions using the 'il' form of the verb.

a) **It's possible to** do more to protect human rights. ➡ **Il est possible de**

b) **It's necessary to** have more council houses. ➡ ....

c) **It's important to** help people who are depressed. ➡ ....

d) **We need to** create new jobs in this town. ➡ ....
   ↳ Use the verb 'falloir' to translate this phrase.

Q3 Traduis les phrases suivantes en **anglais**.

a) L'inégalité entre les gens les plus riches et les gens les plus défavorisés est un <u>souci</u> mondial. ← *'Souci' means the same as 'inquiétude'.*

b) J'adore habiter dans un quartier diversifié. C'est pourquoi je suis pour l'immigration, parce que j'aime connaître les différentes cultures.

c) Il y a plein de réfugiés dans le monde qui ont dû quitter leur pays à cause de la guerre.

Q4 Translate this passage into **English**.

> Ma ville était très industrielle dans le passé, mais depuis que la grande usine a fermé, il y a peu d'emplois. Les hauts niveaux de chômage ont causé une augmentation* du nombre de SDF qui vivent dans la rue. Il faut créer plus d'entreprises avant que la situation s'empire**.

*une augmentation = an increase   **s'empirer = to get worse

When you've finished, check:
☐ Flow — does it sound natural in English?
☐ Tenses — have you translated the different past tenses correctly?

Section 5 — Lifestyle and Social & Global Issues

Contributing to Society

Q1 Translate the sentences below into **English**. Before you start, underline all the nouns. The first four have been done for you.

Remember that nouns can be made up of more than one word.

a) <u>Claude</u> apporte ses <u>ordures</u> au <u>centre de recyclage</u> chaque <u>semaine</u>.

b) Aurélie ne prend plus de bains parce que cela gaspille* de l'eau.
*gaspiller = to waste

c) J'utilise des sacs en papier, car les sacs en plastique endommagent l'environnement.

d) Je ne mange pas de viande parce que ça contribue au réchauffement de la Terre.
↖ Which English word does this remind you of?

Q2 Translate the sentences below into **French**. The verbs in bold should be translated using 'pour + infinitive'.

Translate 'to raise money' as 'collecter des fonds'.

a) Tomorrow, Jules will sing with his choir **to raise** money.

b) Georges does campaigns **to combat** poverty.

c) My sixth form gives money each year **to help** charities.

d) My sister was a volunteer in Africa. She went there **to build*** a school.
*to build = construire ↖ You don't need to translate 'a' into French here.

Q3 Translate this passage into **English**. Before you start, answer the questions below.

> À mon avis, <u>il est</u> très important de s'engager politiquement. La semaine dernière, je suis allé au centre-ville avec mes parents où il y avait une manifestation* pour soutenir les droits des réfugiés. Il faut que le gouvernement <u>fasse</u> quelque chose pour les aider.

*manifestation = protest

a) How will you translate 'il est'? ....

b) Which word shows that the speaker is male? ....

c) Which phrase triggers the subjunctive 'fasse'? ....

Q4 Translate this passage into **French**.

> I want to do something to help society, so I will soon become a volunteer for a charity which aims to* clean up our area. I will spend two hours a week in the forest collecting** rubbish. I would like to do it more often, but I don't have enough time at the moment.

*to aim to = avoir pour but de   **collecting = à ramasser

Before you start, check:
- Time expressions — do you know how to translate them all?
- Tenses — there are a variety of tenses in the passage. Do you know which tenses to use?

Section 5 — Lifestyle and Social & Global Issues

Global Events

Q1 Translate the adverbs in bold into **French**. The first one has been done for you. Then translate each sentence.

The word order might need to change when you translate the sentences into English.

a) Est-ce que tu es ......**déjà**...... allé à la Coupe du monde? **(already)**

b) Mon frère regardait .... des matchs de foot. **(always)**

c) Le festival d'Édimbourg n'a pas .... commencé. **(yet)**

d) Camille regarde .... les Jeux olympiques. **(still)**

You'll have to reuse an adverb from earlier in this question here.

Q2 Circle the verb in brackets that is needed to form the perfect tense verb in each sentence below. The first one has been done for you. Then translate the sentences into **French**.

You don't need to translate 'Wimbledon' or 'Tour de France'.

a) The race **took place** in London in April.   ((avoir) / être)

b) They **went** to Wimbledon last month because they love tennis.   (avoir / être)

c) We **arrived** too late, so we couldn't watch the athletics tournament.   (avoir / être)

d) This year, an English person **won** the Tour de France.   (avoir / être)

Translate 'English person' as one word.

Q3 Translate this conversation into **English**.

a) **Sabine:** Daniel, es-tu déjà allé à un festival de musique?
   Daniel: Bien sûr. Je suis fana de métal, donc je suis allé à un festival l'année dernière. J'ai rencontré beaucoup de gens intéressants.

b) **Sabine:** Dans trois mois, j'espère aller à Barcelone où il y aura un grand concert de pop. Tu serais bête de ne pas m'accompagner!
   Daniel: Ça ne me dit rien. Cet événement sera une perte de temps.

Daniel had his outfit ready for the metal festival.

Q4 Translate this passage into **French**.

You'll need to use 'à' here in French.

International events are very important because they help to create good relationships between countries. Today, I saw a poster for an American jazz festival in my town in July. I don't normally listen to jazz, but I'm going to go to this festival. I hope to find some American friends there.

You'll have to change the word order of this in French.

When you've finished, check:

☐ Articles — have you included them all? Pay close attention to the articles next to plural nouns.

☐ Adjectives — do the adjectives agree with the nouns they're describing?

Section 5 — Lifestyle and Social & Global Issues

Mixed Practice

Q1 Translate this conversation about problems in society into **French**.

Kévin: The number of homeless people in this country is a big problem and it has become worse recently.

Rania: Yes. Poverty has increased* because of the bad state of the economy. What could we do to help?

Kévin: I am a volunteer for a charity which gives out free food. We need more help in the kitchen. You could help us if you wanted.

Rania: I would love to help you. ← Which 'you' will you use here? Read the previous sentence to help you decide.

*to increase = augmenter

Q2 Translate the sentences below into **English**.

a) Hier j'ai mangé trop de bonbons et cela m'a fait vomir.

b) Je détestais le sport. Pour garder la forme, je marchais au lieu de prendre la voiture.

c) Certains régimes qui sont à la mode en ce moment sont mauvais pour la santé.

d) On dit que manger plus de fruits et de légumes peut empêcher certaines maladies.

Q3 Translate this passage into **English**.

> J'ai déménagé dans une grande ville il y a un mois, mais je ne peux pas supporter* tout le bruit. Je ne trouve pas le sommeil quand je me couche le soir à cause de la circulation. La pollution m'inquiète aussi parce que j'ai souvent de la difficulté à respirer**. Je crois que je vais devenir malade.

*supporter = to bear   **respirer = to breathe

Q4 Translate these sentences into **French**.

a) Seven years ago, there was a serious earthquake in Japan. More than one hundred countries and charities helped the victims.

b) Next week, there will be an international protest against war. Many people believe that the government should try to prevent violence between countries.

— Translate 'protest' as 'une manifestation'.

c) My sister used to work for a charity. She helped people in poor countries who had had to leave their homes after a hurricane*. She gave them food, water and clean clothes.

*a hurricane = un ouragan

Section 5 — Lifestyle and Social & Global Issues

Mixed Practice

Q5 Translate this passage into **English**.

You won't use the same tense to translate this into English.

> La nature est ma passion. Quand je <u>finirai</u> mes études, je chercherai un emploi avec une association caritative qui protège l'environnement. Je suis dégoûté quand je vois des images à la télé d'oiseaux de mer couverts de pétrole. Si je pouvais faire quelque chose pour améliorer la situation, je me sentirais plus heureux.

Q6 Translate this passage into **French**. [EDEXCEL]

> In 2015, my friend Inès and I went to London to watch the rugby. It was a global sports event which brought together* people from all the corners of the world. We had had a good journey on the plane, but when we arrived in London the air was very polluted. It was really unpleasant.

*to bring together = rassembler

Q7 Translate this advice from a doctor's waiting room into **English**. [AQA & EDUQAS]

a) Buvez-vous de l'alcool avant de dormir? Selon l'évidence, si vous en buvez moins le soir, vous dormirez mieux.

b) Avez-vous essayé d'arrêter de fumer dans le passé? Avez-vous échoué à cause d'un manque d'aide? Demandez des conseils à votre médecin.

c) Si on mange trop de graisse saturée*, on augmentera le risque d'une crise cardiaque**. Si vous n'êtes pas sûr comment manger équilibré, lisez ces informations.

*la graisse saturée = saturated fat   **la crise cardiaque = heart attack

Q8 Translate this public notice into **French**.

> There is a campaign to raise awareness about* gangs in this area. Police officers are warning that they could be very dangerous. A few days ago, some girls harassed an old lady and then stole her money. <u>The police</u> would be grateful for your help. Look after your neighbours and stay vigilant**.

"Harass me all you want, Morris, you're not stealing any more of my chips."

*to raise awareness about = sensibiliser le public à   *This takes the third person singular form of the verb in French.*
**to stay vigilant = rester vigilant

Section 5 — Lifestyle and Social & Global Issues

Mixed Practice

Q9 Translate these comments about how people would change their local area into **English**.

a) **Angela:** Si j'étais maire, j'installerais plus de fontaines à eau pour donner aux sans-abri un meilleur accès à l'eau potable.

b) **Marine:** J'organiserais un festival de musique, car il n'y a pas assez d'activités pour les jeunes. Ce serait bon pour l'économie locale aussi.

c) **Nawal:** À mon avis, cette ville a besoin de plus de pistes cyclables parce qu'il faut réduire la circulation. La pollution de l'air est dangereuse pour ceux qui habitent ici.

Q10 Translate this passage about drug addiction into **English**. *(AQA & EDUQAS)* — This verb comes from the adjective 'ivre' ('drunk').

> Mon frère était toxicomane*. Il se droguait et il s'<u>enivrait</u> tous les jours. À cause de son addiction, il a beaucoup maigri. Toute ma famille pensait qu'il aurait besoin de soins** de longue durée. Cependant, maintenant il va beaucoup mieux. Il ne se drogue plus et il a un nouvel emploi.

*le toxicomane = a drug addict   *le soin = care

Q11 Translate these sentences into **French**. — Translate this using the phrase 'laisser le robinet ouvert'.

a) I <u>used to</u> use a lot of water. I <u>used to</u> <u>leave the tap running</u> when I was brushing my teeth. After having participated in a recent campaign, I now know how to save water.

b) Dennis has always believed that recycling is important. He says that it's our responsibility to help the planet by recycling all that we can.

c) I often find a lot of rubbish in the park. It is disgusting when people throw it everywhere! I always put my rubbish in the bin. We should respect nature and keep the park clean.

Q12 Traduis ce passage en **français**. — You don't need to translate the underlined words into French. Treat 'WWF' as a masculine noun.

> The <u>WWF</u> is a charity that works with governments to protect animals that are in danger. In 2007, the organisation started an event called <u>Earth Hour</u>, which took place on the last Saturday of March. The aim* was to combat climate change** by asking people to switch off their lights and not use electricity for one hour.

*an aim = un but   **to combat climate change = combattre le changement climatique

Section 5 — Lifestyle and Social & Global Issues

Section 6 — Travel and Tourism

Where to Go

Q1 Complete the French sentences with the correct prepositions. The first one has been done for you. Then translate the sentences into **English**.

a) Joaquim et moi voudrions voyager ......**en**...... Espagne.

b) Nos grands-parents vont .... États-Unis cette année.

c) Cet hiver, je vais passer les vacances .... Chine.

d) Tu vas aller .... Écosse le week-end prochain?

e) Mon frère veut leur rendre visite .... <u>pays de Galles</u>.

This is a singular country even though it looks like it's plural.

Paula had got fed up of holidays at the seaside.

Q2 Translate these sentences into **French**.

You'll need to use the correct form of 'aller' in each of these sentences.

a) Evan and his friends go to England in the summer.

b) Ellie is going to France with her boyfriend, but I'm going to Belgium.

c) My cousins and I went to the countryside together.

d) Lots of people go to Switzerland every year.

e) I'm going to go <u>to London</u> in November.

Remember — if you're talking about going to a specific town or city, you need to use 'à'.

Q3 Translate this passage into **English**. Before you start, make sure you can answer the questions.

Will this phrase be singular or plural in English?

> L'année dernière, je suis allée en Italie avec ma famille. Nous avons passé cinq jours à Rome et puis une semaine au bord de la mer. <u>C'étaient les meilleures vacances</u> de ma vie! Cependant, cette année nous n'allons pas <u>à l'étranger</u>, parce que c'est trop cher.

How many words will you need to translate this into English?

Q4 Translate this extract from a travel blog into **French**.

This word is the same in French (it's masculine).

> I love Africa! I've visited twelve African countries and it is a beautiful <u>continent</u>. Morocco* is my favourite country because the people are very kind and friendly. Next month I will go to Tunisia, where you can swim in the Mediterranean.

*Morocco = le Maroc

When you've finished, check:

☐ Tenses — have you used the correct tenses? There are three different ones in this passage.

☐ Sense — does each sentence make sense when you re-read it?

Accommodation

Q1 Translate these sentences into **French**. Before you start, underline the verbs that you will need to translate using the infinitive. The first one has been done for you.

a) I'm going <u>to look for</u> a small hotel.

b) My father prefers to sleep in a tent.

c) Lucie likes going camping.

d) We can stay in a youth hostel.

Q2 Translate these complaints about accommodation into **English**.

a) On ne peut pas se détendre dans une colonie de vacances. Il y a trop de gens et de bruit.

b) Je suis <u>descendu</u> dans un hôtel de luxe, mais ma chambre était sale. ← The verb 'descendre' means 'to go down', but it can also mean 'to stay'.

c) Il y a un trou dans ma tente. Quand il pleut, il pleut à l'intérieur aussi!

Q3 Translate the comparisons in bold into **English**. The first one has been done for you. Then translate the whole sentence.

a) Les chambres d'hôte sont **plus chères que** les campings. ▷ ......**more expensive than**......

b) Le camping était **moins confortable que** l'hôtel. ▷ ....

c) Les dortoirs sont **aussi propres que** la chambre de famille. ▷ ....

d) La caravane ne coûtera pas **autant que** le gîte*. ▷ ....

*le gîte = holiday cottage

Q4 Translate the following conversation between friends into **French**.

Translate 'stay' as 'loger' in this question.

a) **Guillaume:** Where will you be staying in Spain?
   Nannette: I will be staying in a youth hostel at the seaside.

b) **Guillaume:** I love youth hostels because you can meet lots of interesting people.
   Nannette: I wanted to go to the holiday camp, but it was full. However, the youth hostel is very <u>cheap</u>, so I <u>saved</u> money.

This is an invariable adjective in French. ↗

You need to use the verb 'économiser' here.

Q5 Traduis ce passage en **anglais**.

> Tout le monde devrait faire du camping cet été. Il y a beaucoup de bons campings* en France qui offrent plein de services <u>y compris</u> des machines à laver et de l'électricité pour les caravanes. Qui ne voudrait pas passer une semaine en plein air, libre de faire ce qu'on veut?

Look at what follows this phrase to work out what it means.

*un camping = a campsite

Section 6 — Travel and Tourism

Getting Ready

Q1 Circle the imperative in each sentence, then translate the sentences into **English**.

a) (Visitons) l'agence de voyages.

b) Choisissez votre logement.

c) Donnez-moi votre pièce d'identité.

d) Réserve une chambre avec un balcon.

e) N'oublions pas nos lunettes de soleil.

f) Faites vos valises maintenant!
   — In this context, 'faire' means 'to pack'.

Q2 Translate these sentences into **French**. Before you start, think about which question word you'll need to use in each sentence.

Don't use 'est-ce que' to translate these questions.

a) Where is your luggage, Sam? — The word 'luggage' is plural in French.

b) When are you going on holiday with your parents?

c) How many tickets do you need to buy, Josie?

d) Why does she have three swimming costumes?

e) How do you put on this sun cream? — Use the verb 'mettre' to translate 'put on'.

For Neil and Hallie, the holiday starts as soon as the shades are on.

Q3 Complete these sentences with the correct conditional tense form of the verb in brackets. The first one has been done for you. Then translate the sentences into **English**.

a) Clara ......**voudrait**...... réserver une chambre du 25 mars au 2 avril. **(vouloir)**

b) Un lit simple est trop petit. Je .... un lit à deux places. **(préférer)**

c) Vous .... réserver une chambre qui donne sur la place. **(aimer)**

d) Nous pensons qu'il .... mieux de loger au centre-ville. **(être)**

e) Mes grands-parents .... une chambre avec climatisation. **(vouloir)**

Q4 Translate this email into **French**.

Look at Q3 for help translating this.

> I would like to book a room with two bunk beds from the 29th of June to the 4th of July. We will arrive at approximately 10pm. Last year, we stayed in a room which overlooked the sea. Would it be possible to stay in the same room again?

When you've finished, check:

☐ Verbs — have you conjugated each verb correctly? Think about the person and the tense.

☐ Times — have you translated the times correctly? Remember that France uses the 24-hour clock.

Section 6 — Travel and Tourism

Getting There

Q1 Translate these sentences into **French**. You'll need to use 'y' in each one.

a) I'm going there by car.
b) Katy went there by motorbike.
c) There are two airports in Paris.
d) You can't go there on foot.

Tip — 'y' normally goes before the verb.

There are two verbs in this sentence, so you'll need to think carefully about where the 'y' will go.

Q2 Complete the French sentences with the correct past participle of the verb in brackets. The first one has been done for you. Then translate the sentences into **English**.

a) Je n'ai jamais ......**voyagé**...... en avion parce que cela me fait peur. **(voyager)**

b) Hamid et Tom sont .... d'Algérie en bateau. **(revenir)**

c) Le voyage en car a .... plusieurs heures. **(durer)**

The word 'car' is a false friend — it means 'coach'.

d) Deux heures plus tard, Anna est .... dans le train. **(monter)**

e) À la gare, nous avons .... 40 minutes. **(attendre)**

Q3 Translate these dialogues into **French**.

Use 'pour' to translate 'to'.

a) **Suzie:** I like travelling by train. The train to London is never late.
Ed: That's true, but I find it too expensive. I have to take the bus.

b) **Alice:** I bought a return ticket, but my train left early. ← *Translate this as 'en avance'.*
Olive: I'm sorry, madam. We will reimburse you the price of the ticket.

c) **Ajay:** I think that cars are more reliable* than trains.
Paul: You're wrong! Cars go too slowly and there are always lots of traffic jams on the motorways.
*reliable = fiable

Q4 Translate this passage into **English**.

> Mon voyage à Montréal était très confortable. Je suis monté dans l'avion à dix heures du matin, et j'en suis descendu sept heures plus tard. Quand j'ai atterri, il était midi au Canada. Après être descendu de l'avion, je suis allé à l'hôtel en autobus. J'ai déjà hâte de* prendre le vol de retour.

Translate this phrase carefully — 'être' doesn't mean 'to be' here.

*avoir hâte de = to look forward to

When you've finished, check:

☐ Accuracy — have you translated the meaning of every word?
☐ Flow — do each of your sentences flow naturally in English?

Section 6 — Travel and Tourism

What to Do

Q1 Translate these sentences about going to the beach into **French**.

a) There are some beautiful beaches in Nice.

b) We can go sailing this afternoon.

c) I want to hire a beach umbrella* today.
*a beach umbrella — un parasol

d) These ice creams are delicious.

e) The sea is warmer than yesterday.

f) Lots of people like to sunbathe.
This is a reflexive verb in French.

Q2 Translate these sentences into **English**. Each sentence includes 'plu', which is the past participle for both 'plaire' (to please) and 'pleuvoir' (to rain).

a) Hier soir, il a beaucoup plu à Lyon.

b) Le jardin zoologique nous a beaucoup plu.

c) La visite au parc d'attractions lui a plu.

d) Quand il a plu, nous sommes allés à la librairie.

You'll need to use the context of the sentence to translate 'plu' correctly.

Watch out — 'librairie' is a false friend in French.

Q3 Complete the French sentences with the correct imperfect tense form of the verbs in brackets. The first one has been done for you. Then translate the sentences into **English**.

a) Ma belle-mère ......visitait...... les sites touristiques à Monaco. **(visiter)**

b) Qui .... à l'aire des jeux avec les enfants? **(aller)**

c) Mélanie et Chloé .... dans la piscine extérieure. **(nager)**

d) Quand j'étais petit, je .... du ski à la montagne. **(faire)**

e) ....-vous le musée du Louvre quand vous habitiez à Paris? **(visiter)**

The Louvre is a famous museum in Paris.

Q4 Translate this advice for visiting Strasbourg into **French**. Use the 'vous' form of the imperative.

a) On the first day, visit the tourist office and ask for a city map.

b) After having found the cathedral, walk to the river.
Translate this using 'jusqu'à'.

c) Take a guided tour in order to discover things to do.

d) Choose a postcard of a famous building.

And if you get lost, sit on the floor and wait for help to arrive.

Section 6 — Travel and Tourism

Q5 Complete the sentences below using the most appropriate word from the box on the right. Then translate the sentences into **English**.

a) Qu'est-ce qu'il y a à faire .... ici .... ?

b) Il a voyagé .... pour trouver le château.

| au-dessus de | ~~ici~~ |
| loin | sur |

c) La cathédrale ancienne se trouve .... la place.

d) Je crois que l'office de tourisme est .... la poste.

Q6 Translate these sentences into **French**. Think carefully about the conjunctions you'll need to translate the words in bold.

a) I tried to speak in French **while** I was on holiday in Paris.

b) They found a good restaurant **as soon as** they arrived.

c) We will go to the market **even if** the weather is bad. ← You'll need to use the verb 'faire' here.

d) **Since** the museum is closed, we're going to the shopping centre. ← Hint — you can't use 'depuis' to translate 'since' in this sentence.

Q7 Translate this advert into **English**. Before you start, answer the questions below.

> Cet été, viens passer une semaine à la nouvelle station balnéaire pour les jeunes. Située sur la côte Méditerranéenne, la station t'offrira l'occasion* d'essayer plusieurs** sports nautiques et de participer aux jeux collectifs. Tu pourras aussi perfectionner un passe-temps, ou apprendre quelque chose de nouveau.

*une occasion = an opportunity   **plusieurs = several

a) What is the subject of the verb 'située'? ....

b) Which tense does the verb 'offrira' use? ....

c) How will you translate 'jeux collectifs'? ....

Q8 Traduis ce passage en **français**.

← Look back at Q2 for a clue on how to translate this.

> I have just been to Brussels* and I liked that city a lot. My brother and I went on a tour and the next day we visited some museums. The model village** was amazing and there were some beautiful gardens. In the evenings you could walk through the town centre. We will return to Brussels next year.

*Brussels = Bruxelles
**model village = un village miniature

Section 6 — Travel and Tourism

Practical Stuff

Q1 Translate each of these problems into **English**.

The verb 'être' is in the subjunctive in this sentence.

a) Mia a raté son train.
b) Il y a une erreur dans l'addition.
c) La douche ne fonctionne pas.
d) C'est dommage que le linge de lit ne <u>soit</u> pas propre.
e) La voiture est tombée <u>en panne</u>.
f) La réparation coûte cher.

Hint — 'une panne' is a breakdown.

Q2 Translate these sentences into **French**. You'll need to use a different negative form in each sentence.

a) There wasn't anyone at reception.
b) Unfortunately, there are no more bikes to hire.
c) I found neither the shower block nor the toilets.
d) The receptionist is doing nothing to help <u>us</u>.
e) There is <u>an hour wait</u> because there are only two waiters.

Where should this pronoun go in the sentence?

Translate this as 'une heure d'attente'.

"There weren't any bikes, so I hired us something else instead..."

Q3 Translate these sentences into **English**. Before you start, write down the tense of each passive construction in bold. The first one has been done for you.

a) Ma valise **a été volée** par un homme. ⇨ ......**perfect passive**......

b) Les touristes **sont aidés** par un agent de police. ⇨ ....

c) Elles **étaient attaquées** par un oiseau à la plage. ⇨ ....

d) Les passeports **seront vérifiés** au contrôle de passeports. ⇨ ....

e) Les bagages **ont été laissés** à la gare routière. ⇨ ....

Q4 Translate this passage into **French**.

Use the imperfect here — you can't use the pluperfect with 'depuis'.

> I <u>had been</u> in Toulouse for three days when my motorbike broke down. What a disaster! I went to a garage near the bed and breakfast, but the repairs <u>were quite expensive</u>. Tomorrow I am going to go to Montpellier. This time, there will not be any more problems!

Before you start, check:
☐ Tenses — think carefully about which tenses you'll need, especially in the first sentence.
☐ Accents — which words will have accents in French?

Look back at Q1 for a clue on how to translate this.

Section 6 — Travel and Tourism

Mixed Practice

Q1 Translate these sentences into **French**.

a) I like to go windsurfing, so I want to book accommodation which is close to the beach.

b) He stayed at a seaside resort where he could sunbathe next to the pool all day.

c) The cathedral was opposite our hotel, so we went on a guided tour when we arrived.

d) I wanted to go to the theme park, but it was too far away from the campsite.

e) The employee at the youth hostel hired some mountain bikes for us.

Q2 Translate these sentences into **English**.

a) Je suis allée en Chine et j'ai visité tous les sites touristiques principaux.

b) Comme il est fana de sports nautiques, il ira sur la côte Méditerranéenne.

c) L'année prochaine, nous ferons un tour en bateau des îles de la Manche.

d) Cette année, je suis allé à Carcassonne, où j'ai visité l'église près du centre-ville.

e) Quand je vais en Allemagne, j'aime bien me promener à la campagne.

f) J'espère qu'il fera beau quand elle ira en Italie. Elle veut voir le volcan à Naples.

Break this phrase down into smaller chunks to help you translate it.

Q3 Stephan is talking to his friend Julianna about his stay in an ice hotel. Translate their conversation into **French**.

Julianna: Did you have fun at the ice hotel, Stephan?

Stephan: It was fantastic! It was very cold, but I had packed lots of clothes in my suitcase.

Julianna: I'm very jealous of you. The photos of your stay are beautiful. — *Translate 'stay' as 'séjour'.*

Stephan: There were some disadvantages. The hotel is always full, so I had to book my room in advance. The journey to the hotel also took a long time.

Q4 Traduis le texte suivant en **anglais**.

Use the tense of this sentence to help you guess what this means.

> Je suis gérant* d'un hôtel au bord d'un lac. Auparavant, c'était très démodé. Maintenant, c'est plus moderne et il est devenu très populaire avec les touristes. Cette année, l'hôtel sera ouvert du 1 février au 31 août. Toutes les réservations faites avant le 1 juin incluront une visite gratuite à l'église voisine.

*un gérant = a manager

Section 6 — Travel and Tourism

Mixed Practice

Q5 Translate these sentences into **French**.

a) I will be travelling to Grenoble to watch the Tour de France, so I would like to book a room with a view of the main road.

b) They have organised a hike for the first day of their holiday. They need to take sleeping bags because they will be camping in the mountains.

c) You can book a package holiday at the travel agents. We chose a holiday that offers a museum tour and two rooms in a famous hotel.

In French, this will be translated as 'organised stay'.

Q6 A tour guide is preparing his group for a trek. Translate the passage into **English**.

> Nous allons voyager à pied de ce village-ci à cette montagne-là. Demain, la température sera de plus de trente degrés, donc je vous ai acheté beaucoup de crème solaire. Mettez-la fréquemment, s'il vous plaît. Vous devriez tous avoir une tente et un sac à dos pour que vous puissiez porter facilement toutes vos affaires.

Q7 Translate these sentences into **French**.

a) My father has never liked going on holiday to hot countries. He hates using the air conditioning in hotel rooms.

b) She loves visiting New York, but she prefers to stay in accommodation where there is no noise.

c) We always used to stay on a campsite in Wales. I didn't like sharing the toilets and the showers with other people, so now we stay in a bed and breakfast.

Q8 Traduis la conversation suivante en **anglais**. [EDEXCEL]

Omaira: As-tu l'horaire pour le métro? Je pense que nous avons raté le dernier train. Qu'est-ce que nous allons faire?

Yvonne: Ne t'inquiète pas, nous pouvons prendre un taxi à l'hôtel.

Omaira: J'aimerais ça parce que ma valise a été endommagée à l'aéroport.

Yvonne: Quel voyage! S'il n'y avait pas eu un retard de quatre heures à l'aéroport, nous serions arrivées beaucoup plus tôt!

This is the conditional perfect tense. It describes things that 'would have happened'.

Section 6 — Travel and Tourism

Mixed Practice

Q9 Translate these sentences into **English**.

a) Cet hiver, nous irons en Finlande. Nous prendrons un avion pour Helsinki, et puis nous louerons une voiture pour aller à la chambre d'hôte à Tampere.

b) L'année dernière, elle est allée en Belgique. Les avions lui font peur, donc elle a décidé de prendre le ferry. Le voyage a duré plus de douze heures.

c) Cet après-midi, je vais en France. Je m'inquiète d'être en retard, donc je veux arriver à la gare au moins une heure avant l'heure de départ.

Q10 Translate this postcard to a friend into **French**.

Remember that in French, the perfect tense can be used to say what someone has been doing.

> It's very hot here in Australia. We have been spending lots of time near the sea where it's more pleasant. Yesterday, Diana went water skiing. Unfortunately*, she fell and had to go to hospital. I am going to visit one of the pink lakes tomorrow. I will send you some photos!

*unfortunately = malheureusement

Q11 Translate these sentences into **English**. [EDEXCEL]

a) Hier, je me suis perdue pendant la visite. Je prenais des photos des bâtiments quand tout le monde est parti sans moi!

b) Il a oublié de composter son billet dans le tram, donc il a dû descendre au prochain arrêt. La prochaine fois, il ne fera pas la même erreur!

c) Ma mère a demandé l'aide d'un agent de police car j'avais mis mon passeport dans mon sac à main que je m'étais fait volé.

After getting separated from his tour group, Clive found himself a long way from home.

Q12 Traduis le texte suivant en **français**.

This is the same word in French, and it's feminine.

> My friend loves visiting Brazil*. Two years ago, she spent three weeks at a campsite in the middle of the jungle. The only way** to get there was to travel on a very narrow road, then to take a boat on the river. In future, she would prefer to stay in a youth hostel.

*Brazil = le Brésil
**a way = une manière

Section 6 — Travel and Tourism

Section 7 — Current & Future Study and Employment

School Life

Q1 Translate these comments about school subjects into **French**.

- a) ICT is a useful subject for young people.
- b) Do you like German?
- c) He finds maths difficult.
- d) She prefers music, but she is not very gifted.
- e) My sister hates art.
- f) Why is physics too complicated?
  — This subject is singular in French.

Don't forget that these subjects will all need a definite article (le, la, l', les).

Q2 Translate these comments about timetables into **English**.

- a) À la rentrée, les cours commenceront à huit heures et demie.
- b) Nous avons histoire-géo deux fois par semaine.
- c) Le cours de biologie dure une heure et quart.
- d) La récréation est trop tard dans la journée.
- e) La directrice a fait un nouvel emploi du temps l'année dernière.

Élise's interest in biology was microscopic.

Q3 Fill in the gap with the correct present tense form of either 'pouvoir' or 'vouloir'. Then translate the sentences into **French**. The first verb has been done for you.

- a) She **is able to** use the computers in her lunch break. ▷ ......**peut**......
- b) We **want** longer holidays in summer. ▷ ....
- c) They **can** take PE lessons on the sports ground. ▷ ....
- d) I **want** to have well-equipped* classrooms. ▷ ....
  *well-equipped = bien équipé

Q4 The passage below has been translated from French into **English**. Fill in the gaps to complete the translation.

> Je voudrais retourner dans mon ancienne école. Ici, les autres élèves me harcèlent. Ils me lancent des injures, mais je ne les écoute pas. Il y a aussi beaucoup de pression parce que nous allons passer un examen le mois prochain.

I would like to go back to my .... Here, the other pupils .... They insult me, but I don't .... There's also a lot of pressure because we're going .... next month.

Q5 Write down the tenses of the verbs in bold. Then translate the sentences about opinions on school into **English**. The first tense has been done for you.

a) Ma mère **a pensé** que l'école privée était mieux. ➡ ......**perfect**......

b) Je **préférerais** avoir moins de devoirs et moins de lecture. ➡ ....

c) On **devra** redoubler si on a de mauvaises notes. C'est injuste! ➡ ....

d) Vous me **mettiez** sous trop de pression pendant mes examens! ➡ ....

Q6 Translate these sentences into **French** using 'il faut'.

Use the verb for 'to get up', without the reflexive pronoun.

a) You must leave your phone at home.

b) You must not talk in the library.

c) We must wear a tie, and we must not wear make-up.
This is a reflexive verb in French.

d) You must raise your hand to speak.

e) You must not run in the corridors.

f) We must not enter the classroom during break.

Q7 Translate this letter from a French penfriend into **English**.

What school subject is this?

> Mon emploi du temps va changer en seconde. J'aurai plus de langues vivantes et je commencerai l'algèbre. J'ai peur que ce soit trop compliqué pour moi, car je trouve que les chiffres* sont difficiles à comprendre. Comme toi, je m'intéresse au chinois, mais le prof est assez sévère. Il m'a déjà donné des retenues.

*un chiffre = a number

Be careful translating this phrase — it includes an indirect object pronoun.

Q8 Translate the following passage into **French**.

> I have studied at a boarding school* for four years. I miss my parents, but my friends have become my family. The teachers were very understanding when I failed an exam, and the headteacher says that he will give the result to my parents at the end of term.

*a boarding school = un internat

When you've finished, check:

☐ Tenses — have you used the right ones? Double-check the first sentence.

☐ Vocabulary — have you spelt everything correctly? Make sure you haven't missed out any letters by mistake.

Section 7 — Current & Future Study and Employment

School Events

Q1 Translate these school event notices into **French**.

a) A ticket for the end-of-year show will cost five euros.

b) There is a parents' evening the night before half-term.

c) On Saturday there will be a charity sale in the gym.

d) The <u>drama group</u> will perform* their play this week.

*to perform = jouer — This noun takes the singular form of the verb in French.

Carl was the star of the drama group, hands down.

Q2 Complete the sentences below using the correct French direct object pronoun for the nouns in brackets. Then translate each sentence into **English**.

Think about the gender and number of the nouns in French to help you choose the correct pronouns.

a) Les élèves ......l'...... utilisaient pendant la fête du sport. **(the swimming pool)**

b) Il va .... visiter pendant l'excursion scolaire. **(the museum)**

c) Notre équipe scolaire d'échecs .... gagnera! **(the tournament)**

d) Elle .... a annulées car les voyages seraient dangereux. **(the school trips)**

Q3 Translate this conversation about a school exchange into **French**.

a) **Cosette:** I loved the Spanish exchange.
   Antoine: Me too! I liked my penfriend and her family a lot.
   Cosette: <u>My favourite part</u> was the trip to the football stadium.

Translate 'my favourite part' as 'what I liked the most'.

b) **Antoine:** I didn't go <u>there</u> because my parents hadn't given me permission*.
   Cosette: You can go <u>there</u> next time. We will return to Spain next year.

*give someone permission = autoriser quelqu'un

You'll need to use 'y' to translate 'there' in these sentences.

Q4 Translate this diary entry into **English**.

How will you translate this phrase?

La rencontre parents-professeurs a eu lieu la semaine dernière. <u>Après avoir discuté</u> de mon bulletin scolaire, j'ai pensé que mes parents seraient de mauvaise humeur parce que j'enfreins* les règles de temps en temps. Cependant, le professeur <u>leur a dit</u> que je vais passer en classe supérieure et <u>cela leur a plu</u>.

*enfreindre = to break — Think about the role of each word in these phrases to help you work out what they mean.

When you've finished, check:

☐ Flow — do your sentences sound natural in English?

☐ Verbs — have you translated the right 'person' for each verb?

Section 7 — Current & Future Study and Employment

Education Post-16

Q1 Translate these sentences into **English**. Before you start, underline the 'avoir...de' construction in each sentence. The first construction has been done for you.

a) Tu <u>as l'intention d</u>'étudier quelles matières?

b) Ils ont l'ambition d'étudier la chimie, mais c'est vraiment difficile.

c) Théo a besoin de trouver un emploi.

d) Je n'ai pas envie* de continuer mes études, car je préférerais travailler tout de suite.

*envie = desire

Q2 Translate the verbs in bold in the sentences below into **French**. The first one has been done for you. Then translate each sentence.

Translate 'military school' as 'école militaire'.

a) We **will go** to military school in September. ⇒ ....irons.................

b) They **will stop** school at the end of year 11. ⇒ ....

Use the 'tu' form for c).

c) You **will be** an apprentice in your father's firm. ⇒ ....

d) In year 13, I **will pass** all my exams. ⇒ ....

e) After his A-Levels, he **will take** a gap year*. ⇒ ....

*a gap year = une année sabbatique

Q3 Translate the following conversations into **English**, thinking carefully about word order and pronouns.

a) **Marcus:** Quelle est l'université la plus proche? Je voudrais y étudier.
   Georgia: Il y en a une en ville. Tu pourrais économiser de l'argent si tu habitais chez toi.

b) **Mikhail:** J'en ai marre de l'école. Je n'irai pas à l'université.
   Dafydd: Ce n'est pas pour tout le monde, mais ton apprentissage sera éducatif aussi.

c) **Bethany:** J'ai toujours voulu <u>monter</u> ma propre entreprise après l'école.
   Sheldon: C'est une idée ambitieuse! Il faut travailler bénévolement au début.

Translate 'monter' as 'to start' in this sentence.

Q4 Translate this pupil's study plans into **French**.

> I would like to study at university but if the level is too difficult, I won't cope. The career adviser told me that you have to be hard-working and intelligent, which worries me. However, my dad really loved university. <u>I need to</u> make a decision soon.

Look back at Q1 for a clue on how to translate this.

Before you start, check:
☐ Reflexives — which verbs will be reflexive in French?
☐ Accents — which words will have accents in French?

Section 7 — Current & Future Study and Employment

Languages for the Future

Q1 Translate these sentences about learning languages into **English**.

Can you guess which language this is?

a) Il voudrait apprendre le gallois.

b) Mon père est bilingue.

c) Si j'avais le temps, j'apprendrais une autre langue européenne.

d) Je trouve que l'alphabet <u>russe</u> est très difficile.

e) On doit pratiquer les langues fréquemment.

f) Les langues changent tout le temps, donc on n'arrête jamais de les apprendre.

Q2 Translate the comparative adverbs in bold into **French**. Then translate each sentence. The first comparative adverb has been done for you.

Remember that adverbs don't agree with the subject of the verb.

a) Foreign languages allow me to communicate **more clearly**. ➡ **plus clairement**

— *Use 'à travers' to translate 'across'.*

b) You can travel <u>across</u> the world **more easily**. ➡ ....

c) I learn other languages **more quickly**. ➡ ....

d) I will be able to work abroad **more frequently**. ➡ ....

e) Fred speaks **more openly*** when he is on holiday. ➡ ....
 *open = franc(he)

Q3 Translate these sentences into **English**. *What does this 'en' refer to?*

a) Je pense que c'est une perte de temps d'apprendre des langues étrangères puisque tout le monde parle anglais. À mon avis, nous n'<u>en</u> avons pas besoin.

b) Mes parents ont appris le latin à l'école, mais personne ne l'utilise pour communiquer! Aujourd'hui, les langues comme le chinois et l'espagnol sont beaucoup plus utiles.

c) À l'avenir, je voudrais être fonctionnaire à l'étranger, donc pour moi les langues vivantes sont les matières les plus importantes.

Q4 Traduis ce passage en **français**.

> I started learning German and Spanish four years ago, but I will have to drop a language next year. I prefer Spanish. If I spoke it fluently*, I would have a better salary and better promotion prospects. By learning more languages when I am older, I will have more choices in my career.

*fluently = couramment

When you've finished, check:

☐ Accuracy — have you translated the meaning of each word?

☐ Tenses — have you identified all the different tenses? Think carefully about the last two sentences.

Section 7 — Current & Future Study and Employment

Applying for Jobs

Q1 Translate these questions about job applications into **French**. Each question should begin with either 'qui' or 'que'.

When 'qui' and 'que' are the object of the sentence, don't forget to invert the verb and the subject.

a) Who did you meet at the interview?
b) What should I write on this form?
c) Who works well <u>in a</u> team?
   Translate this as 'en' here.
d) Who doesn't have experience?
e) What do you know about our business?
f) What do I have to do to apply?

Q2 Complete the sentences below using the correct French translation of the phrases in brackets. Then translate each sentence into **English**. The first one has been done for you.

a) Je ......**viens de recevoir**...... une réponse. **(have just received)**

b) Tu .... ta candidature à ce poste. **(have just applied)**

c) Gabrielle .... sa lettre de candidature. **(has just sent)**

d) Sam .... l'annonce pour son emploi idéal. **(had just seen)**

e) Ils .... l'école. **(had just finished)**

You'll need to use the imperfect tense of 'venir de' in these last two sentences.

Q3 Translate this application letter into **French**.

If you don't know this word, do you know the word for 'business'?

> I read a job advertisement on your website. I would like to apply for the position of secretary in your <u>company</u>. Last month I finished some work experience in an office, which has given me the necessary experience. I could start straight away.

Ned was overcome by job hunting blues.

Q4 Translate this extract from a job interview into **English**.

a) **Émile:** À votre avis, quelles qualités doit-on avoir pour ce poste?
   Michel: Il faut être chaleureux et confiant. J'ai toutes les compétences <u>dont</u> vous avez besoin.
   How will you translate 'dont' into English?

b) **Émile:** Et pourquoi avez-vous posé votre candidature à ce poste?
   Michel: Je voudrais avoir un emploi qui est plus passionnant que le mien.

c) **Émile:** Depuis combien de temps travaillez-vous dans cette industrie?
   Michel: Depuis dix ans. J'ai fait un stage ici il y a des années et j'ai beaucoup appris.

Section 7 — Current & Future Study and Employment

Career Choices and Ambitions

Q1 Translate these sentences into **French**.

Remember that in French, you don't need 'un' or 'une' when you're talking about what somebody does.

a) I would like to be an interpreter because you can earn lots of money and live abroad.

b) My best friend is going to become an artist. She liked art in school, so now she is following her dream.

c) I want to be a mechanic because I like cars. In the future, I will work for a famous brand.

Lee couldn't wait to work on some more complicated vehicles.

Q2 Translate these sentences into **English**. Before you start, circle the correct tense of the verb in bold. The first verb has been done for you.

a) Pendant son enfance, Sophie **a voulu** / (**voulait**) devenir ingénieure.

b) La semaine dernière, ma mère **a quitté** / **quittait** son emploi.

c) Quand il avait vingt ans, mon grand-père **a été** / **était** maçon.

d) Vincent **a travaillé** / **travaillait** comme policier pendant cinq ans.

Q3 Translate this passage into **French**. Before you start, answer the questions below.

> I have had a part-time job since last year. I work <u>as a waitress</u> in a restaurant on Saturdays. It's not exciting, but <u>there aren't many</u> job prospects* in this town and <u>I get on well with</u> my manager**.

*a job prospect = un débouché   **a manager = un(e) gérant(e)

a) How will you translate 'as a waitress'? ....

b) How will you translate 'there aren't many'? ....

c) What type of verb will you need to translate 'I get on well with'? ....

Q4 Traduis ce passage en **anglais**.

The word 'métier' means the same thing as 'emploi' and 'boulot'.

> J'ai toujours rêvé de devenir journaliste parce que c'est un <u>métier</u> très enrichissant et je pourrais voyager. Cependant, je ne sais pas si cette carrière serait pratique. Quelquefois il est difficile de trouver des postes journalistiques et je préférerais travailler dès que* j'ai fini mon bac.

*dès que = as soon as

Before you start, check:
- [ ] Flow — identify any tricky bits that will need rephrasing in English.
- [ ] Conjunctions — do you know how to translate them all?

Section 7 — Current & Future Study and Employment

Mixed Practice

Q1 Translate these sentences into **French**.

  a) After her A-Levels, Flora will spend two months abroad to improve her French.

  b) If he gets good marks, he will study medicine because he would like to be a nurse.

  c) I could have a part-time job while I study, in order to get more experience.

  d) Ella wants to take a gap year. She worked hard during her exams, so she should relax.

  e) My parents think that I should do further studies*, but I want to be an apprentice plumber.
  *further studies = les études supérieures (f)

Q2 Translate this passage into **French**.

This is the same word as 'strong' in French. (pointing to 'loudly')

> Drama is my favourite subject because the lessons are really interesting. Normally, it is forbidden to talk loudly in class, but during drama lessons we can make a lot of noise. I will study drama in sixth form college. I believe that I'm very gifted, so I would like to become a famous actor.

Q3 Translate this job interview into **English**. *(EDEXCEL & EDUQAS)*

This is the noun form of the verb 'vendre'. (pointing to 'vente')

  Loïc: Pouvez-vous vous présenter?

  Marc: Bien sûr. Je m'appelle Marc et je m'intéresse beaucoup à la vente.

  Loïc: Je vois dans votre CV que vous avez peu d'expérience professionnelle.

  Marc: C'est vrai, mais j'ai fait un stage dans un centre commercial il y a un an.

  Loïc: Pourriez-vous étudier pour une licence en même temps que travailler?

  Marc: Absolument. J'étudiais deux soirs par semaine dans mon ancien travail.

Q4 Traduis cette annonce en **anglais**.

> Le Lycée du Roi Graham se présentera au public mercredi prochain. Venez voir nos bâtiments modernes et notre grand terrain de sport pendant notre journée portes ouvertes*. Nous avons les meilleurs résultats du pays. Commencez votre carrière idéale chez nous, où vous obtiendriez les notes dont vous avez toujours rêvé!

*une journée portes ouvertes = an open day

Section 7 — Current & Future Study and Employment

Mixed Practice

Q5 Translate the following passage into **French**.

> At the start of the year, I had a bad school report. However, after the school exchange, I improved my French mark because my penfriend and I had spoken in French all week. Being able to talk with <u>people abroad</u> is a valuable skill, so I was very happy.

Translate this phrase using one word.

Q6 Translate the following conversation about careers into **English**.

Julia: Dans ma carrière, je veux donner un exemple à suivre. J'espère devenir quelqu'un de célèbre, comme chanteuse ou mannequin. Je ne pourrais jamais être professeur.

Yanic: Moi non plus. On aurait trop de devoirs à corriger et trop de cours à enseigner. Pourtant, ma carrière idéale serait différente de la tienne. Je ferais du travail bénévole.

Julia: Aurez-vous besoin d'étudier pour le faire?

Yanic: Non. Je pense que l'expérience comptera plus que les diplômes.

Q7 Translate these comments about school life into **French**.

a) Normally I follow the school rules, but there are some pupils in my school who bully others. At university, the students will behave better.

b) Since I live far from school, I get up at six thirty in the morning. Now I always wake up early, which could be useful for work.

c) I used to go to a state school*. The teaching was very good and the career adviser helped me to find an apprenticeship.
*a state school = une école publique

Q8 Translate this passage into **English**.

This doesn't actually mean 'a little job' — what else could it be?

> Hier j'ai commencé <u>mon petit job</u> comme maître nageur* à la piscine. Je mets de l'argent de côté pour payer mes études aux États-Unis. Je gagnais de l'argent en faisant du baby-sitting pour mes profs, mais j'ai voulu avoir un emploi plus régulier. J'ai l'intention de partir dans deux ans.

*un maître nageur = a lifeguard

Section 7 — Current & Future Study and Employment

Mixed Practice

Q9 Translate these conversations with a career adviser into **French**.

Translate this as 'à l'intérieur'.

a) **Luc:** I don't want to go to university or work indoors. What should I do?

Henri: If you like being in the open air, you could do an apprenticeship in gardening.

b) **Layla:** My best subjects are maths and physics. I have always understood them.

Henri: You could become an engineer. You will have to study chemistry too.

c) **Henri:** It's important to choose a career that you like. What do you want to do in the future?

Zoé: I like music and my teacher says I'm quite gifted, but the lack of* jobs worries me.

*a lack of = un manque de

Q10 Translate the following passage into **English**.

> Mon père est informaticien. Ma mère ne travaillait pas, mais elle vient de commencer un nouvel emploi dans un magasin. Ils veulent que j'aille à l'université parce qu'ils n'ont pas eu l'occasion* d'obtenir une licence eux-mêmes. Je me sens obligé de le faire.

*une occasion = an opportunity

Q11 Translate these job adverts into **English**.

a) Nous cherchons quelqu'un pour faire la vaisselle dans notre restaurant. Vous devez être travailleur et ponctuel. Les entretiens auront lieu la semaine prochaine.

b) Voudriez-vous un emploi à mi-temps après l'école? On a besoin d'assistance à la bibliothèque publique. Le salaire est raisonnable et vous pouvez prendre des pauses.

c) Le poste de secrétaire dans notre bureau sera disponible* à partir de janvier. Le candidat idéal aurait au moins deux ans d'expérience et un diplôme au niveau bac.

*disponible = available

Use the rest of the sentence to guess what this phrase means.

Q12 Translate this diary entry into **French**.

> Two days ago I got a detention because I had fallen asleep during my chemistry lesson. I'm always tired at the moment because I'm taking extra classes* in the evenings to study fashion. If I fail my exams, I will have to retake and I will not be able to follow my plan for next year.

*an extra class = un cours supplémentaire

Kyle could fall asleep pretty much anywhere.

Section 7 — Current & Future Study and Employment

Answers

The answers to these questions are sample answers only, just to give you an idea of how they might be translated. There may be different ways to translate the sentences and passages that are also correct.

Section 2 — Me, My Family and Friends

Page 7 — About Yourself

Q1 a) I come from Manchester.
b) sont — My neighbours are of Swiss origin.
c) habite — I live in London, in the south of England.
d) s'appelle — My cousin is called Félix.
e) Êtes — Are you British, sir?
f) est — Your date of birth is the 7th of August 1980.

Q2 a) Je m'appelle Yang.
b) Mon anniversaire est en novembre.
c) J'ai dix-sept ans.
d) Il est né au pays de Galles.
e) Ma mère est belge.
f) Nous avons une grande maison.

Q3 a) I was born in Glasgow, in Scotland.
b) Imperfect — When I was six (years old), I lived in Paris.
c) Imperfect — My parents used to live in the United States.
d) Present — We come from Spain.

Q4 My name is Priya and I'm sixteen (years old). My birthday is the fifteenth of January. I'm French and I come from Paris, but I came to Great Britain a year ago with my family. We have been living in London for ten months.

Page 8 — My Family

Q1 a) J'ai deux sœurs et un frère.
b) You — Tu habites / Vous habitez près de (chez) tes / vos grands-parents.
c) She — Elle est fille / enfant unique.
d) We — Nous habitons avec mon père et sa petite amie / copine.

Q2 a) Our nephew is called Léo.
b) mes — Here are my cousins, who are called Jean-Luc et Daniel.
c) son — He likes / loves his twin brother a lot.
d) ma, mon, ma — I live with my mother, my step-father and my half-sister.

Q3 a) My sister married / got married to her girlfriend yesterday.
b) est mort — His / Her father died last year.
c) se sont séparés — Your grandparents separated in 1998.
d) ont divorcé — My uncle and my aunt (got) divorced three years ago.

Q4 Demain c'est l'anniversaire de mon beau-père. Nous allons dîner dans un restaurant italien en ville. Mon frère aîné ne veut pas venir, alors / donc il restera à la maison / chez nous pour s'occuper de / garder nos sœurs, qui sont des jumelles.

Q5 We live for a long time in my family. My grandfather is ninety-two (years old), and he is still / always in good health. My grandmother died at the age of eighty-eight. The secret to their long life? They never argued / used to argue, even when they were young.

Page 9 — Describing People

Q1 a) Il a les cheveux raides et marron / bruns.
b) red — Elle porte des lunettes rouges.
c) green, wavy — Nous avons les yeux verts et les cheveux ondulés.
d) long — Tu as / Vous avez une longue barbe.
e) short, blonde, blue — J'ai les cheveux courts et blonds et les yeux bleus.
f) tall — Les filles sont très grandes.

Q2 a) I am shorter / smaller than my brother.
b) less ugly than — She is less ugly than me.
c) more hair than — Maurice has more hair than Frédéric.
d) fewer spots than — He has fewer spots than before.
e) as short as — His / her hair is as short as mine.

Q3 a) Your two sons are very tall for their age.
b) particulièrement — I knew that you were talking / speaking because your voice is particularly loud.
c) trop — All of my friends tell me that I speak too quickly, but I don't agree.
d) vraiment — My older sister doesn't like the fact that she really looks like / resembles our father.

Q4 Pensez-vous que la Joconde est belle? Elle a les cheveux longs et bruns / marron, ni raides ni bouclés. À mon avis, elle est moins jolie que les mannequins d'aujourd'hui. Mais ce qui est intéressant, c'est son air mystérieux. On veut savoir ce qu'elle s'imaginait.

Page 10 — Personalities

Q1 a) I am nice / kind / likeable and chatty, and sometimes lazy too.
b) can't tell — Usually I'm funny, but I'm shy sometimes.
c) male — I am quite selfish, and a bit annoying too.
d) female — People say I'm clever / intelligent, because I work hard.

Q2 a) Nous sommes très sportifs / sportives.
b) Les personnes âgées sont toujours bavardes.
c) Tes / Vos oncles ne sont jamais heureux / contents.
d) Les filles sont trop bruyantes.

Q3 a) She has a fun / funny personality.
b) sensitive — My best friend can be very sensitive.
c) nice / kind — You are really nice / kind and open(-minded).
d) understanding — My brother should be more patient and understanding.

Answers

Q4 Ma mère / maman est travailleuse et généreuse. Elle a toujours été gentille / sympa / aimable, et elle n'a jamais été égoïste. Même quand / lorsque je suis pénible / agaçant(e) / embêtant(e), elle n'est pas injuste. Tout le monde l'adore.

Q5 When I was little, I was very reserved so I didn't have many friends. Generally, my friends thought that I was too sensitive. I'm still quite shy, but I have (some) friends now who are more like me. They are a lot more understanding.

Page 11 — Pets

Q1 a) Did you (use to) have a pet?
b) recevais — I used to receive (some) tropical fish (for) every birthday.
c) aimait — Tom didn't use to like horses.
d) était — My best friend always used to be / was always my dog!

Q2 a) Aimez-vous / Aimes-tu tous les gros animaux?
b) old — Ma tortue est très vieille et fatiguée.
c) white — J'ai une souris blanche qui s'appelle Trixie. Elle est très méchante!
d) beautiful — J'ai deux cochons d'Inde gris. Ils sont beaux.

Q3 pets; told me that; at the moment; I would have

Q4 Avez-vous vu notre chat Marvin? Nous ne l'avons pas vu depuis vendredi dernier. Il est noir et il a des pattes blanches. Je m'inquiète / suis inquiet / inquiète parce qu'il n'aime pas être (tout) seul. Nous pensons qu'il est dans un garage ou sous une voiture. Téléphonez-nous si vous le trouvez. Il nous manque!

Page 12 — Style and Fashion

Q1 a) Guillaume wants to become a fashion designer / stylist in the future.
b) vont — The famous models go to London in September.
c) sais — I know what's in fashion at the moment.
d) faites — Do you make all your handbags from / out of leather?

Q2 a) Les pantalons serrés sont devenus à la mode l'année dernière.
b) ai acheté — J'ai acheté un jean chic hier.
c) a perdu — Le mannequin a perdu sa montre hier soir.
d) a mis — Il a mis sa robe de chambre à la fête.

Q3 a) What is your size, sir?
b) Quels — Which / What kinds of shoes are currently in fashion?
c) Quelle — Which / What colour of hat is your favourite?
d) Quelles — Which / What are your favourite brands?

Q4 After getting dressed, I started to do my make-up. I applied my lipstick, but I couldn't / wasn't able to choose which jewellery to wear. Normally, I wear a T-shirt and jeans when I go out. However, I decided to wear a dress for this party.

Page 13 — Relationships

Q1 a) My grandfather doesn't help me to do my homework any more.
b) ne, jamais — People say that / It is said that teenagers never respect their parents.
c) n', pas encore — You still haven't sent the gift to your cousin. *Or* You haven't sent the gift to your cousin yet.
d) n', personne — There isn't anyone / There is no-one in my family with whom I have a good relationship.

Q2 You should have ticked a), b) and f).
a) Ma meilleure copine / amie Sara se dispute souvent avec sa sœur.
b) Max s'entend avec son frère.
c) Je ne connais pas vraiment mes cousins.
d) Ton / Votre frère ne parle plus à ton / votre beau-père.
e) J'aime sortir avec mes copains / amis.
f) Mon père et moi, (nous) nous entendons bien.

Q3 a) She got angry with her mother yesterday.
b) nous sommes amusé(e)s — We had fun together at the party.
c) s'est occupée de — My sister looked after her niece last weekend.
d) s'est fait — Louis made friends easily on holiday.

Q4 J'ai de mauvaises relations / mauvais rapports avec ma sœur. Nous ne nous entendons pas bien. Elle se dispute toujours avec moi, et elle ne m'écoute jamais. Nos parents ne comprennent pas, parce qu'elle est polie devant eux. Hier elle a volé mon argent de poche. Je ne l'aime pas du tout!

Page 14 — Socialising with Friends and Family

Q1 a) Nos parents aiment aller à la piscine.
b) en — Mes amis / copains jouent au foot en ville.
c) chez — Ta / Votre sœur reste chez Siobhan.
d) de — Il revient de la fête de Gethin.

Q2 a) You go swimming with Ali on Monday evenings.
b) souvent — My best friend often visits me.
c) il y a deux mois — A new café opened near the library two months ago.
d) tous les jours — I talk to / with my mother every day.

Q3 a) Jouer aux jeux de société avec ma famille est ennuyeux.
b) Aller à la plage est une bonne façon / un bon moyen de passer du temps ensemble.
c) Apprendre une nouvelle compétence ensemble a vraiment amélioré notre amitié.
d) Faire du vélo avec mon père est agaçant. Il va trop vite.

Q4 I want to attend a music festival with two friends, but my father won't let me / allow me to go (there). I don't want to argue with him, but it's not fair!

Answers

Q5 J'ai rencontré ma meilleure amie / copine Solange il y a douze ans. Nous sommes comme des sœurs. Nous avons les mêmes intérêts, et je peux lui parler de tous mes problèmes. L'année dernière elle est venue en Grèce avec ma famille et nous espérons y retourner après nos examens.

Page 15 — Partnership

Q1 a) Ma cousine va **habiter** avec son petit ami / copain après Noël.
b) Je veux **choisir** ma bague de fiançailles.
c) Mes parents ont décidé de **se séparer** cette année.
d) De nos jours / Aujourd'hui la majorité des gens peuvent **se marier** parce que le mariage pour tous existe dans beaucoup de pays.

Q2 a) My wedding will be very extravagant.
b) nous séparerons — I hope that we will never break up / separate.
c) adoreras — You will love him / her forever. *Or* You will always love him / her.
d) épousera — He will marry the man of his dreams.
e) divorceront — It is likely / probable that his / her parents will divorce / get divorced.

Q3 Le mariage n'est pas pour tout le monde. Beaucoup de gens se marient pour plaire à leurs parents. À mon avis, il n'est pas nécessaire de se marier pour être heureux / heureuse / content(e). Je voudrais avoir des enfants à l'avenir, mais en ce moment je pense que mon éducation est plus importante.

Q4 What / Such fantastic news, my brother is going to get married! I'm very happy about it because I get on well with his girlfriend, or rather, with his fiancée! And I know that they are very much / really in love, so I believe that the marriage will last. They have been living together for six months, and they will get married / marry next year.

Page 16-18 — Mixed Practice

Q1 a) My sister is the person who supports me the most. She is always there for me.
b) The annoying girls who / that you (have) described, are they your cousins? I don't like them.
c) We have eight grandchildren who will visit us next week.
d) My aunt Nora is nearly always angry. We don't get on well.
e) Théo hasn't spoken to his step-mother since their argument six months ago. I think it's sad.

Q2 Cette semaine, vous aurez besoin de patience quand / lorsque vous rencontrerez un ami / copain. Vous serez très fier / fière d'un(e) membre de votre famille mercredi, qui est plus fort(e) que vous pensez. N'oubliez pas le bel étranger que vous avez rencontré la semaine dernière, parce qu'il a un cadeau pour vous.

Q3 a) He comes from Belgium but his family emigrated to Wales when he was six (years old).
b) At the age of ten, people used to call me / called me "Wiggy" because I had very long hair.
c) I never answer questions about my age. In my opinion, they are impolite.
d) My parents intend to move to Spain when I am older.

Q4 a) **Tanvir:** Il est important d'être ouvert et honnête avec ton / votre mari / époux ou ta / votre femme / épouse.
Audrey: Je suis d'accord. Mon mari / époux est très compréhensif et il m'écoute.
b) **Nkenna:** Essayez de vous entendre avec la famille de votre partenaire. *Or* Essaye / Essaie de t'entendre avec la famille de ton / ta partenaire.
Fergal: Oui, j'essayerai. Je demanderai l'avis / l'opinion de la sœur de ma femme sur les noces.
c) **Freda:** Est-il nécessaire d'être le meilleur ami / copain de votre / ton partenaire? *Or* Est-il nécessaire d'être la meilleure amie / copine de votre / ton partenaire?
Peter: Oui, ma petite amie / copine ne passait jamais du temps avec moi, alors / donc nous nous sommes séparés.

Q5 a) Even if you're an independent person, to be happy you have to find friends who share your interests and your hobbies.
b) My parents work hard during the week, so they try to spend time together by attending a dance class on Saturday evenings.
c) To celebrate our birthdays, my friends and I have dinner in restaurants.
d) My neighbours participate / take part in charity activities as a family to help those who are less privileged than themselves.

Q6 Quand / Lorsque j'ai rendu visite à ma grand-mère récemment elle m'a montré des photos de son mariage / ses noces. Elle était très belle à l'âge de dix-neuf ans. Elle avait les cheveux blonds et les yeux verts. Mon grand-père était grand et fort, et elle dit qu'il était le meilleur mari / époux du monde. Ils se sont mariés il y a cinquante-cinq ans.

Q7 Marie-Antoinette was of Austrian descent but she became the queen of France in the 18th century. She lived in luxury in a big palace / castle at Versailles, near Paris, while most French people were living / lived in poverty. She died on the sixteenth of October, 1793, but she is still well known today.

Q8 **Élodie:** Il doit être difficile d'avoir des animaux (domestiques) et un travail / emploi aussi.
Gérard: Oui. J'ai un chien, mais mon grand-père s'occupe de lui quand / lorsque je suis au travail.
Élodie: Je voudrais bien avoir un chien, mais ma belle-mère y est allergique. Quel serait ton animal domestique idéal, si tu avais le choix?
Gérard: Je voudrais un cheval, mais je sais que c'est impossible pour moi. Les chevaux sont trop chers!

Q9 a) Je m'appelle Ed et j'ai dix-huit ans. J'ai les cheveux bouclés / frisés et châtain et les yeux bruns / marron foncés. Je suis intelligent et amusant / drôle / rigolo / marrant.

Answers

b) Je m'appelle Lucie. Je suis timide avec les gens que je ne connais pas bien, mais quand / lorsque tu feras ma connaissance tu verras que je suis aimable, patiente et généreuse.

c) Je suis Sophie. J'étais une personne très sérieuse. Maintenant, je dirais que je suis plus sociable. Mes amis / copains pensent que j'ai un très bon sens de l'humour parce que je les fais rire.

Q10 **Jérémy:** I won't wear my suit tomorrow. It doesn't suit me.
Sadiq: It's our sister's wedding! You'll have to wear something smart / stylish!
Jérémy: She'll be too busy to argue with me about my clothes.
Sadiq: If you don't wear it, I will ignore you all day / for the whole day.
Jérémy: That would be really unfair. Why can't you support me?

Q11 a) Mon frère et ma meilleure amie / copine se marieront / vont se marier cet été et je suis très heureux / heureuse / content(e) pour eux. Le mariage sera / les noces seront en Italie parce qu'elle est italienne.

b) Les gens parlent / On parle trop de l'amour. J'en ai marre, parce que c'est le sujet de tous les livres que je lis et tous les films que je regarde.

c) Mehdi avait une petite amie / copine l'année dernière, mais ils se sont séparés. Il a décidé qu'il ne se mariera jamais.

Q12 When I met my half-brother, he had already had everything that I had wanted when I was young. I thought that he was spoilt. Despite that, we have always got on well. We are very different in appearance. For example, he is bald, and in comparison, I have a lot of black curly hair.

Section 3 — Technology, Free Time and Customs & Festivals

Page 19 — Technology

Q1 a) I would like a new MP3 player.
b) devez — You must click on the link (in order) to view the article.
c) sait — He doesn't know how to download images.
d) avez éteint — Have you turned off the computer?
e) doit — You mustn't sit (down) too close to the screen.

Q2 a) Cet ordinateur portable était un cadeau de mon cousin / ma cousine.
b) ce — Allumez / Allume ce lecteur DVD.
c) ce — Nous avons trouvé ce nouveau logiciel vraiment utile.
d) Cette — Cette console de jeux est très chère.

Q3 a) Est-ce que tu as / vous avez cassé l'imprimante? J'ai besoin d'imprimer ces photos pour mon frère.
b) Je n'ai plus besoin de ces courriers électroniques / (e-)mails. Est-ce que tu peux / vous pouvez les effacer / supprimer?
c) Est-ce que je peux taper mon message en utilisant l'écran tactile? Je le préfère au clavier.

d) Est-ce que tu m'as / vous m'avez envoyé un texto? Je ne l'ai pas reçu.

Q4 I go on the Internet all the time. It helps me a lot with my homework because I can find all the information that I need. I send emails to my pen friend too. I used to use my tablet to access the Internet, but it stopped working four days ago.

Page 20 — Social Media

Q1 a) Noémie always uses social networks to talk to her aunt.
b) jamais — He never uses chat rooms / forums because he thinks they're too dangerous.
c) Récemment — Recently, he has started sharing more information on the Internet.
d) déjà — He has already uploaded all the photos of his holiday. **Or** He has already put all the photos of his holiday online.

Q2 de messages; j'ai peur du; être un ami / un copain; harceler.

Q3 a) **Addie:** I (really) like social media. I used it to chat to Arnaud last week.
Darci: Me too. Have you seen the video from / of his birthday party? He has uploaded it / put it online.
b) **Paige:** He wrote a sports blog. Did you read it?
Serge: No, I needed to create an account to read it, but I didn't know how to do it. Can you show me the blog?

Q4 J'utilise les réseaux sociaux tous les jours. Ils me permettent de rester en contact avec les membres de ma famille que je ne vois pas très souvent. Cependant / Pourtant, mon frère aîné dit que je devrais faire attention à ce que je partage sur les médias sociaux. L'année dernière, quelqu'un a volé des informations de son compte et il est devenu victime de vol d'identité.

Page 21 — Music

Q1 a) They play the piano after school.
b) She played — She played the trumpet at the concert.
c) I used to play / I was playing / I played — I used to play / I was playing / I played the guitar in a band.
d) We will play — We will play the saxophone at the party.

Q2 a) Je connais **quelques** chanteurs / chanteuses doué(e)s.
b) J'aime **toutes** les chansons sur ce CD.
c) J'ai écouté **quelques** chansons à la radio.
d) **Chaque** matin, je joue de la clarinette.

Q3 a) When I was at primary school, I used to like / I liked playing the flute.
b) avaient — Their parents bought them a violin when they were ten (years old).
c) faisions — We were / used to be part of an orchestra before going to university.
d) allait — He used to go to all the concerts, but now he doesn't have enough money.

Answers

Q4 a) Lucille: J'ai toujours adoré la musique rap. J'aime l'écouter quand / lorsque je fais mes devoirs.
Nicolas: Moi aussi. J'ai acheté un nouvel album de rap il y a deux jours. C'est génial / formidable / chouette!

b) Jérôme: J'étais fana de musique rock, mais maintenant je la trouve embêtante / pénible / énervante.
Agathe: Je déteste la musique rock aussi. Elle m'énerve. À mon avis, le meilleur genre de musique est le disco parce que les chansons sont vraiment animées / vivantes.

Q5 Last weekend, I went to a classical music concert. Before going there, I had never listened to classical music. The orchestra was incredible and some pieces of music were sung by a great choir. I liked the concert a lot, therefore / so I will buy a ticket for the one next year.

Page 22 — Cinema and TV

Q1 a) Normally, my parents prefer to watch the news during breakfast.
b) chercher — He's going to look for a soap opera with a more interesting story.
c) trouver — Before finding this documentary, I only watched cartoons.

Q2 a) J'aime regarder les films romantiques avec mon petit ami / copain.
b) films de guerre — Mon oncle a regardé deux films de guerre à la télé hier soir.
c) film policier — Ils / Elles m'ont dit que c'est leur film policier préféré.
d) films d'animation — Elle adore regarder les films d'animation.

Q3 a) The horror film (that) I saw yesterday was very frightening.
b) qui — I prefer (the) adverts that make me laugh.
c) que — The TV channel (that) I like broadcasts game shows.
d) qui — He is the actor who plays the main character.

Q4 Île de Glace
Après avoir regardé la bande-annonce passionnante, je suis allé(e) au cinéma pour regarder ce film d'action avec ma sœur. Les effets spéciaux au début étaient fantastiques, mais l'histoire était trop difficile à suivre. J'étais très déçu(e).

Page 23 — Hobbies and Role Models

Q1 a) As she loves art, she paints each / every day.
b) donc — His / Her cousins wanted to go skiing, so they went to the mountain(s).
c) comme — He only reads books as he is very interested in reading.
d) donc — I really like playing board games, so my father bought me some.

Q2 a) Il fera de l'athlétisme si tu joues / vous jouez au rugby.
b) Even if — Même si c'est difficile, je voudrais pratiquer l'escrime.

c) since — J'ai décidé de faire du tir à l'arc puisqu'il semblait être un sport passionnant.
d) but — Elle avait beaucoup de passe-temps intéressants, mais maintenant elle ne fait rien.
e) because — Il m'inspire parce qu'il est un joueur d'échecs fantastique.

Q3 Élodie has been collecting stamps since childhood. She loves travelling, so she tries to find stamps that represent all the countries that she has visited. A year ago, she also started to collect foreign coins.

Q4 Mon modèle est un photographe célèbre qui prend des photos d'animaux. Je passais beaucoup de temps chez moi / à la maison, mais il m'a encouragé(e) à sortir en plein air avec mon appareil photo. D'habitude, je prends des photos de la campagne. J'espère le rencontrer un jour.

Page 24 — Food

Q1 a) They eat a lot of seafood.
b) trop de — I try not to eat too many biscuits.
c) un peu de — He always adds a bit of salt to his meals.
d) assez de — She doesn't eat enough vegetables.
e) trop de — You (have) added too much pepper.
f) peu de — There is little fish in this soup. **Or** There isn't much fish in this soup.

Q2 a) Elle n'aime pas le chou. Elle pense que c'est dégoûtant.
b) J'adore — J'adore le saumon. Si je pouvais, je mangerais du poisson tous les jours!
c) J'aime beaucoup — J'aime beaucoup la cuisine / nourriture indienne parce qu'elle est / c'est épicée / piquante.
d) il déteste — Sa mère cuisine souvent de la dinde, mais il déteste ça.

Q3 a) il ne mange que / il mange seulement
b) des fruits sucrés
c) proper future tense
Mon frère est très difficile. Il refuse de manger des légumes et il mange seulement / il ne mange que des fruits sucrés comme les fraises ou les ananas. Il mange beaucoup de gâteaux et de biscuits aussi. Il ne mangera jamais bien et cela m'inquiète.

Q4 My grandmother grew up in Italy, a country well known for its cooking / food. When I visit her, we cook pasta with garlic and tomatoes. It's her birthday next week and, as a present, I will prepare roast chicken in a mushroom sauce. My parents are going to make a chocolate cake.

Page 25 — Eating Out

Q1 a) All the dishes on the menu were very expensive.
b) a donné — The waitress gave him a dirty plate.
c) est partie — She left before finishing her meal.
d) a servi — The coffee wasn't hot enough when it was served to us.

Q2 a) Serveuse: Voudriez-vous commander un dessert, madame?
Cliente: Oui, je voudrais une tranche de gâteau et l'addition, s'il vous plaît.

Answers

Answers

b) **Client(e):** Je ne sais pas ce que je veux. Recommanderiez-vous ce vin?
Serveur: Voulez-vous le goûter? Je peux vous en apporter une bouteille.

Q3 a) I like going to Chinese restaurants because they serve meals that I don't know how to cook myself.
b) salés — My parents went to a seafood restaurant. My father liked it a lot, but my mother found the dishes too salty.
c) pratique — My friends and I love tapas restaurants because we can share the dishes. It's very practical.

Q4 Samedi, nous sommes allés à un restaurant français. Mon ami / copain a commandé la soupe comme entrée / hors d'œuvre. Il a pensé que c'était très amer. Pour mon plat principal, j'avais commandé un steak / bifteck bien cuit, mais ce n'était pas assez chaud. Nous avions encore faim quand / lorsque nos desserts sont arrivés. Heureusement, ils étaient parfaits!

Pages 26-27 — Sport

Q1 a) Je nage plus mal quand / lorsque je suis fatigué(e).
b) Elle croit qu'elle court le mieux.
c) À mon avis, il a mal joué.
d) Il joue au foot(ball) le plus mal.
e) Nous savons que nous avons bien joué.
f) Ils / Elles s'entraîneront mieux demain.

Q2 a) They do (rock) climbing at the sports / leisure centre.
b) la — I practised sailing when I was on holiday.
c) le — She used to practise badminton when she was eleven (years old).
d) de la — I would go swimming if I had someone to come with me.

Q3 Dans le passé / Auparavant ; au sport; après avoir; l'équitation

Q4 a) He practises five sports, and he must train hard for each one.
b) quelqu'un — I play volleyball with someone who lives near me / my house.
c) tout le monde — The player who scored the goal is better than everybody.
d) quelque chose — You / We must do something to support the competitors.

Q5 a) At the moment, she trains twice a day.
b) s'entraîneront — Next year, the athletes will train on the sports field.
c) m'entraînais — I used to train with the school team on Mondays.
d) t'entraînerais — Would you train with me before the race?
e) s'était entraîné — Lance had trained very hard before the competition.

Q6 a) Je ne joue pas au tennis parce que je trouve ça ennuyeux.
b) ne...plus — Ils / Elles ne regardent plus le sport à la télé.
c) ne...jamais — Notre famille n'a jamais aimé l'athlétisme.

d) ne...ni...ni — Elle ne fait ni de l'équitation ni du cyclisme / vélo.

Q7 Last year, I went to Canada with my sister to watch a skiing competition. We've been following this sport for almost six years. Skiing is more exciting to watch than other winter sports. When I'm older, I would like to learn to ski.

Q8 Mon frère est joueur de basket(ball) professionnel depuis qu'il a vingt ans. Il a toujours été très doué en sport. C'était très embêtant / agaçant / énervant quand / lorsque nous étions petits. D'habitude, je devais tricher pour gagner un jeu. Maintenant, je ne suis pas très sportif / sportive, mais j'aime faire du patinage sur glace / du patin à glace le week-end.

Pages 28-29 — Customs and Festivals

Q1 a) Next Friday is going to be a bank / public holiday.
b) allons célébrer — We are going to celebrate Epiphany / Twelfth Night.
c) vais participer — I am going to take part in the processions.
d) vont emballer — They are going to wrap all the presents.

Q2 a) Dans mon pays, on ouvre les cadeaux de Noël le 25 / vingt-cinq décembre.
b) En France, on fête / célèbre la fête des mères le dernier dimanche de mai.
c) On porte des costumes fantastiques pour Mardi Gras.
d) La fête du travail / Le premier mai, on vend des fleurs dans les rues.
e) On joue de la musique toute la journée pendant le carnaval.

Q3 a) I think Easter is great because the festival takes place in spring, and spring is the best season of the year!
b) For me, Easter is a very religious festival. I go to church with my parents and then we visit our close family.
c) I'm fed up with / I've had enough of Easter. The festival has become too commercial and people / we have forgotten its real meaning.

Q4 L'hiver dernier, je suis allé(e) en Suisse pour le Nouvel An. J'y suis allé(e) pour rendre visite à mes cousin(e)s qui habitent à Genève. Pour eux / elles, le 31 / trente-et-un décembre est un jour important, parce que les gens de cette région fêtent / célèbrent un événement célèbre dans l'histoire de Genève. Nous sommes allé(e)s à un concert spécial dans la cathédrale.

Q5 a) **Gascon:** Where will you celebrate Eid al-Fitr this year, Ibrahim?
Ibrahim: This year, I will go to Morocco where my grandmother lives.
b) Que
Gascon: What will you do to celebrate it?
Ibrahim: In the morning, we will go to the mosque to pray. In the evening, all the family will eat together.

Answers

c) Comment
Ibrahim: How do you celebrate / are you celebrating Christmas?
Gascon: My mother is Jewish and she doesn't celebrate it. However, my father is Christian. He wants me to go to midnight mass.

Q6 a) La Toussaint est plus animée / vivante au Mexique qu'en France.
b) moins...que — Notre fête de village est moins populaire que la fête du travail.
c) autant...que — Pour le premier avril, les enfants français essayent / essaient de mettre autant de poissons en papier que possible sur le dos de leurs amis / copains.
d) aussi...que — La Saint Valentin n'est pas aussi importante que la fête nationale.

Q7 Il y a un mois, Louisa est allée en France pour fêter / célébrer Noël avec sa petite amie / copine, Camille. La veille de Noël, elles ont dîné avec sa famille, puis elles ont ouvert des cadeaux. Cette année, elles veulent le fêter / célébrer chez elles. Louisa voudrait faire un gâteau de Noël.

Q8 On the 21st of June, it's the 'Fête de la Musique' throughout France. I went there with my friends three years ago. This year, we'll be playing music on stage. I'm scared of singing in front of the spectators, but I know that it will be an incredible experience.

Pages 30-32 — Mixed Practice

Q1 In July, we invite you to a festival which will celebrate all forms of music, including jazz and opera. The concerts will be open to everyone, so don't hesitate to visit our website (in order) to buy (some) tickets. If you want more information, send an email to the following address.

Q2 Fabien: What are you preparing for dinner this evening, Simone?
Simone: I wanted to prepare some beef in a pepper sauce, but I have no meat. I am going to have to prepare something else.
Fabien: I'm going to an Italian restaurant. You could come with me.
Simone: That's a great idea! We can share the bill.

Q3 a) Après avoir quitté son travail, mon père a commencé à chercher de nouveaux passe-temps. Il a trouvé un club de pêche sur Internet. Son vieil ami James est aussi membre du club.
b) Dans son temps libre, Élodie aime jouer aux jeux vidéo. Elle a récemment acheté une nouvelle console de jeux. Elle peut l'utiliser pour enregistrer des vidéos et pour les partager avec ses amis / copains.
c) Il y a deux ans, j'ai reçu une liseuse électronique pour mon anniversaire. Avant, je lisais de vrais livres, mais ils n'étaient pas très pratiques.

Q4 a) Mon ami / copain a mis en ligne quelques photos du match de hockey.
b) Suivez / Suis notre blog pour lire toutes les actualités / informations sportives / de sport.
c) Les footballeurs / joueurs de foot(ball) ont partagé quelques vidéos des meilleurs buts du tournoi.
d) Elle n'a pas regardé le match, mais son ami / copain lui a envoyé le résultat.
e) Je vais surfer sur Internet et chercher la date de chaque course.
f) Quand / Lorsque je tchattais avec Sadie sur Internet, elle a dit qu'elle ne pouvait pas venir au match.

Q5 Étienne: I'm hungry. Do you want to order something to eat? I saw an advert on social media for a new pizzeria.
Aishah: Is there a menu that we can download? I'd like to know if there are any chicken pizzas.
Étienne: Yes, I've already downloaded it on my tablet. There are a lot of meat pizzas and the prices are very reasonable.

Q6 Samedi prochain, j'irai au cinéma avec mon cousin / ma cousine pour regarder un film d'horreur. L'histoire a lieu dans un château au milieu d'une forêt. Mes chanteurs préférés ont écrit la musique. Mon cousin / Ma cousine les déteste, mais je suis fana de leurs chansons. Ce sera génial / formidable!

Q7 a) Three months ago, they went to a Christmas market in Normandy where they bought lots of regional foods like cheese and seafood.
b) What I prefer is the cake that we / people make for Epiphany / Twelfth Night. When I was younger, I used to help my mother to make it before the festival / celebration.
c) At Hanukkah, we / people prepare potato pancakes. At my house, everyone loves them. Last year, my sister had eaten twenty of them before dinner!

Q8 Le modèle de Katrina est un acteur dans un nouveau film qui sortira le mois prochain. Elle adore regarder ses films parce qu'il est très doué. Elle le respecte aussi parce qu'il travaille plus dur que d'autres acteurs. Sa mère a acheté des billets pour le film en ligne. Ils étaient assez chers, mais Katrina veut vraiment regarder le film.

Q9 a) Each year, there is a surfing festival in Biarritz. Lots of tourists come to see the surfers because they're very exciting to watch.
b) Last year, I went to an extreme sports festival with my friend. He's been doing extreme sports for more than eight years, and he took part in the skateboarding competition.
c) Next winter, we will travel to Québec to go to the winter carnival. There will be lots of sporting events during the carnival, including canoeing on ice!

Q10 a) Dans mon émission de télé préférée, un fermier nous montre comment cultiver les légumes à la maison / chez nous. Cela semble assez facile, mais je pense que ce serait difficile.
b) Il y a quelques années, Neema a participé à un concours à la télé où elle a fait des dizaines de petits gâteaux.
c) Une actrice à la télé a écrit un livre de recettes pour montrer que faire des repas sains n'est pas aussi compliqué qu'il (le) semble.

Answers

Q11 Last weekend, I went to the badminton world championship. I was sitting (down) far away from the court, but there was a big screen which helped me watch the match. It was very interesting because the umpires made decisions during the matches using the cameras in the stadium.

Q12 Cet après-midi, je suis allé(e) à un café qui vient d'ouvrir au centre-ville. La propriétaire est une actrice d'une émission de télé pour les enfants. Quand / Lorsque j'étais petit(e), je la regardais tout le temps. Malheureusement, les serveurs étaient tous très impolis et la nourriture / cuisine était affreuse. Je n'ai pas laissé de pourboire.

Section 4 — Where You Live

Page 33 — Where You Live

Q1
a) It's a village near (to) Calais.
b) au bord de — We live by the sea / at the seaside.
c) en face du — The town hall is opposite the bridge.
d) au-dessus de — My flat / apartment is above the swimming pool.
e) à côté de — His / Her office is next to the bakery.
f) dans — They live in the same block of flats / building / apartment block.

Q2
a) Est-ce qu'il y a / Y a-t-il un grand centre commercial dans ton quartier?
b) nos — Il y a une rivière / un fleuve entre nos maisons.
c) son — Yasmin habite derrière son école primaire.
d) Ma — Ma ville n'a pas de stade.
e) ses — André n'aime pas ses voisins.
f) leur — Il y a des arbres devant leur immeuble.

Q3 Je n'aime pas habiter dans une station balnéaire. En été, il y a trop de touristes, alors / donc il y a beaucoup de circulation. En hiver, il n'y a rien à faire / il n'y a pas de distractions. S'il y avait plus de transports en commun, je visiterais d'autres lieux / endroits.

Q4 I've lived in the country(side) for ten years, but I would like to live in town because it's more lively. It's too quiet here. In my ideal town / city, there would be lots of good shops, a cinema and a leisure centre. I would live in the town / city centre and I would go everywhere on foot / walk everywhere.

Page 34 — The Home

Q1
a) We live in a beautiful detached house.
b) I live in a semi-detached house with my boyfriend.
c) Gretel's family lives on the second floor.
d) Do you live in council housing / a block of council flats / on a council estate?
e) We have a very green garden which has lots of pretty flowers.
f) Fabien and Noémie used to live / were living / lived in an average / medium-sized house on a typical street.

Q2 étais; habitions; devais; avons déménagé; avais

Q3
a) Dans notre appartement il y a trois salles de bains et une petite cuisine.
b) house, windows — Ma maison idéale aurait de grandes fenêtres pour voir le soleil.
c) house, dustbin, cellar — Votre / Ta maison est assez propre / rangée, Henri, mais j'ai trouvé une poubelle sale dans la cave.
d) catastrophe — Il y a un problème avec le four et j'ai besoin de faire le dîner. Quelle catastrophe!

Q4 If you had lots of money, what kind of house would you buy? Lots of rich people don't buy a beautiful castle, but (they) prefer to find a more modest house. Often they want to improve it themselves, by adding a swimming pool or a gym in the basement, for example.

Page 35 — Home Life

Q1
a) I eat breakfast at half past six / six-thirty.
b) parfois — Xavier does the cooking sometimes.
c) jamais — You never tidy your room!
d) Normalement — Normally it's my sister who sets the table.
e) Le vendredi soir — On Friday evenings, I clean the bathroom.
f) Le week-end — At (the) weekend(s), my parents do some gardening.

Q2
a) Nous nous sommes levé(e)s à sept heures ce matin.
b) present — Je me lave chaque jour / tous les jours.
c) present — Vlad se couche assez tard.
d) imperfect — Émilie se réveillait tôt pendant les vacances.
e) imperfect — Quand / Lorsque j'étais enfant, je m'habillais très lentement.

Q3
a) **Marie:** (Personally,) I walk the dog to earn my pocket money. It's great!
b) **Julien:** I wash our / the neighbours' cars if the weather is nice / if it's a nice day. It's not too difficult.
c) **Diana:** I have to help my father to do (some) DIY on Saturday mornings. I find it tiring.
d) **Akmal:** I like it when Amélie teaches me how to prepare meals.

Q4 Aujourd'hui, c'était la fête des mères, donc / alors nous nous sommes levés tôt pour lui faire le petit déjeuner au lit. Pendant que notre mère dormait, mon frère a acheté des croissants, et (moi,) j'ai préparé du café. Puis nous avons fait toutes les tâches ménagères comme (nous faisons) chaque année, parce qu'elle a besoin de se détendre.

Pages 36-37 — Shopping

Q1
a) Do you like this black dress?
b) ce — I love these cotton trousers.
c) Ces — These hats are old-fashioned.
d) ces — I would like to try on these trainers.
e) cette — Where did you buy this shirt?
f) ce — Have you got these jeans in grey?

Q2
a) Thursday is market day.
b) The deli(catessen) sells the best meat.
c) Personally / As for me, I go to the bakery every morning to buy some bread.
d) There's a good fishmonger's / fish shop in town.

Answers

    e) Did you buy this cake at the cake shop?
    f) We do the shopping / go shopping at the supermarket because it's less expensive.

Q3 **a)** Achetons du café pour demain matin. Je voudrais un paquet de biscuits aussi.
    b) Je n'ai pas de sel, je suis désolé(e). Mais si vous voulez / tu veux du poivre, je peux vous aider / t'aider.
    c) Je vais acheter un kilo de pommes de terre pour le dîner. Avons-nous / Est-ce que nous avons de l'ail aussi?
    d) Cette tranche de gâteau était délicieuse. Est-ce qu'il y avait / Y avait-il de la confiture au milieu?

Q4 **a)** Il pense que ce manteau est en cuir.
    b) Tu dois / Vous devez acheter un nouveau jean.
    c) C'est combien, cette écharpe en soie? *Or* Cette écharpe en soie coûte combien?
    d) J'aime le pull en laine en vitrine.
    e) Ce blouson / Cette veste est sale. Je ne vais pas l'acheter.
    f) Ces chaussures sont trop petites. Il a besoin de la pointure 40 / quarante.

Q5 **a)** I can't refund you without your receipt, madam.
    b) The shop assistant refunded me because of the damage.
    c) The belt was broken, so Louis got a refund / was refunded.
    d) If the customer says they want (to get) a refund / to be refunded, you must / we must do it.

Q6 **a)** Il / Elle / Ça te va, Philippe.
    b) m'allait — Cette robe ne m'allait jamais.
    c) lui vont — Les jupes longues ne lui vont pas du tout.
    d) me va — Est-ce que ce maillot de bain me va?
    e) lui vont — Ces chaussures lui vont.

Q7 **Christophe:** I want two hundred grams of mushrooms and a cabbage, please.
    Stallholder: There you are, sir.
    Christophe: Give me some more mushrooms.
    Stallholder: Is that enough?
    Christophe: Yes, there are enough of them now. How much does that cost?
    Stallholder: Three euros and forty-nine cents, sir.

Q8 Je préfère choisir mes fruits et mes légumes moi-même au marché, où la nourriture / l'alimentation est fraîche. S'ils ont l'air bon, j'en achèterai beaucoup. Mes parents prenaient leur temps aux magasins comme la boucherie, parce qu'on devrait toujours essayer de trouver de bons ingrédients.

Q9 My friend Lili and I often buy clothes together. She really knows what suits me, and I give her advice on her purchases too. Recently she persuaded me to buy an extravagant yellow dress. Next weekend she's going to help me (to) choose a new outfit in the sales.

Page 38 — Directions

Q1 **a)** Take the second road on the left.
    b) Descendez, tournez — Go down the street and then turn right.
    c) Suivez — Follow the signs for the church.
    d) Tournez — The railway station? Turn to your right.
    e) Traverse — Cross the river.
    f) Continue — Continue straight on, as far as the corner.

Q2 **a) Tourist:** Comment puis-je / (est-ce que) je peux trouver la mairie / l'hôtel de ville?
    Mayor: Traversez le pont, puis suivez les panneaux.
    b) Child: Excusez-moi, où est le commissariat?
    Adult: Viens avec moi, ce n'est pas loin. Traversons la rue.
    c) Actor: Aidez-moi, s'il vous plaît! Je cherche le théâtre.
    Busker: Tournez à gauche au carrefour et c'est à coté de la banque.

Q3 **a)** vous
    b) imperfect
    c) jusqu'à
    Pour votre entretien, venez à notre bureau au centre-ville. L'entrée est située / se trouve en face du bâtiment qui était la poste. Entrez et prenez l'ascenseur jusqu'au troisième étage. Tournez à gauche et allez (jusqu')au bout du couloir.

Q4 It's easy to find my house, don't worry. At the bus station, take the number fourteen bus. Get off in front of the library, and turn left at the traffic lights. Near (to) the enormous tree you will see a green house. Even if you get lost on the way, you will cope. See you soon!

Page 39 — Weather

Q1 **a)** Il y a du vent dans le sud-est.
    b) Il neige — Étienne, regarde! Il neige!
    c) il pleut — À Rouen il pleut beaucoup.
    d) Il y a du brouillard — Il y a du brouillard à Nantes.
    e) il fait froid — Delphine dit qu'il fait froid aujourd'hui.

Q2 **a)** In Cannes, the weather will be sunny during the film festival.
    b) fortes — In the north, there will be clouds. In the south, there will be heavy rain.
    c) orageux — After a stormy morning, there will be bright / sunny spells by the sea / at the seaside.
    d) couvert — The sky was overcast last Monday, as usual in England in the month of January.
    e) pluvieuse — The rainy season is coming to Mexico, therefore / so the tourists are going to leave the country.

Q3 **a)** S'il fait beau dimanche, ils / elles joueront au tennis.
    b) S'il pleut cet / cette après-midi, je ne quitterai pas la maison.
    c) S'il fait chaud pendant le week-end, nous irons à la plage.

Answers

d) S'il neige ce soir, l'école / le collège n'ouvrira pas demain.

Q4 Je voudrais habiter en Espagne un jour, puisqu'il y a un climat doux. Je déteste l'hiver dans ce pays. L'année dernière il a neigé chaque jour / tous les jours pendant trois semaines! Il fera plus chaud en Espagne qu'ici. J'aime le tonnerre et les éclairs lorsqu' / quand il y a un orage, mais je préfère le soleil.

Pages 40-42 — Mixed Practice

Q1 Hier j'ai essayé d'acheter un nouveau manteau. J'ai cherché dans tous les grands magasins, mais tous les manteaux étaient trop grands. Puis il a plu pendant que j'attendais l'autobus. J'en avais marre! Je vais essayer encore demain quand / lorsque je ferai les courses au supermarché.

Q2 a) In Nancy, there is a smart flat / apartment with two bedrooms, (which is) a three minute walk from the town / city centre. You would be able to relax in the garden during the summer.
b) In February, we sold this charming house, situated in the suburbs, very close to the church. There was a big bedroom with a balcony.
c) This (bed)room would be ideal for a student or a single person. It's a furnished room in the town / city centre. The heating is not included.

Q3 Tibault: Qu'est-ce que tu penses de ce parfum? Je pense que je l'achèterai.
Coralie: Ce serait un excellent cadeau pour ta petite amie / copine.
Tibault: Je suis d'accord. Où veux-tu / est-ce que tu veux aller maintenant?
Coralie: J'espérais aller essayer le pull que nous avions vu plus tôt.
Tibault: Bonne idée. Il t'allait bien.
Coralie: Je veux trouver aussi une cravate pour mon père, et peut-être des chaussettes amusantes.

Q4 Hi Benoît! We have been here in Switzerland for two days, in my aunt's new house. She has a big fireplace in the living room. It's great! It snowed during the night, so this morning all of the countryside looked like a Christmas card. If it's sunny tomorrow, we will go to the frozen lake.

Q5 Finally, spring has come. The snow has melted, the sun has arrived and it's warmer on the coast. Today would be a good day to wash the car or do a spring clean. The sky will still be overcast / There will still be overcast skies in Vichy, but next week it will be nice everywhere.

Q6 a) La patinoire est assez loin. Prenez la première sortie de l'autoroute, et puis c'est la deuxième route à droite.
b) Vous cherchez le commissariat? Tournez à gauche aux feux et allez / continuez tout droit. Après avoir traversé la place, vous le verrez.
c) Selon votre carte, vous avez déjà passé la gare, mais la carte n'est pas correcte / juste. C'est là-bas, sur la colline.
d) Pour aller à la bijouterie, descendez la rue et traversez le pont. C'est tout près. Pourrais-je vous la montrer?

Q7 a) I have always dreamed of a detached house, far from the town / city centre, because my parents used to live in the countryside.
b) The house must have at least four bedrooms, two bathrooms and lots of windows.
c) I would also like to live close to a bus stop to go into town easily and go shopping with my friends.
d) I want to live abroad one day, where I could have my own outdoor swimming pool. I will have to become very rich!

Q8 J'en ai marre de mon fils. Le week-end il dort jusqu'à midi et puis il se couche vraiment tard. Il ne m'aide jamais à nettoyer la maison, et hier il a laissé des assiettes sales partout dans la cuisine. Il ne me manquera pas lorsqu' / quand il déménagera l'année prochaine!

Q9 Located behind the town hall, the new market opened on Saturday. It sells regional specialities and international products at very reasonable prices. Would you like to try our food? This Sunday, every customer will receive a free bag of cherries, and there will be a 30% reduction on our tins of duck pâté this week!

Q10 Lena: Je suis désolée, mais je vais être en retard. Je me suis disputée avec ma mère.
Paul: Pourquoi vous êtes-vous disputées?
Lena: Je ne pouvais pas trouver mon porte-monnaie, alors / donc elle m'a fait ranger ma chambre avant de sortir.
Paul: C'est injuste! *Or* Ce n'est pas juste!
Lena: Exactement! Je suis vraiment en colère, et maintenant il y a un embouteillage! Rendez-vous / Rencontre-moi à 11 heures.
Paul: Bien sûr. Je t'attendrai devant le musée.

Q11 a) Nous devons / Il faut avoir un grand jardin, car j'adore regarder les fleurs pendant les après-midi ensoleillés. Avoir deux jardins serait idéal. L'un derrière la maison et l'autre devant.
b) À mon avis, la chose la plus importante est une grande cuisine, où on peut faire des repas chauds lorsqu' / quand il fait froid dehors / à l'extérieur.
c) Si nous avions une belle chambre avec beaucoup d'armoires pour les vêtements de mon / ma partenaire, ce serait parfait. Dans notre ancienne maison, il y avait des vêtements partout!

Q12 Check your purchases at the till before leaving the shop, and keep the receipt. If you discover a problem with your clothes, you must tell us so that we can reimburse you / give you a refund. Later on, if you decide you don't like the products, we will only offer you an exchange.

Section 5 — Lifestyle and Social & Global Issues

Page 43 — Healthy Living

Q1 a) My parents really prefer to walk.
b) rarement — Didier rarely does (any) exercise.
c) certainement — I will certainly eat more fruit in the future.

Answers

d) sainement — In sixth form / (secondary) school, we are taught to eat healthily.

Q2 a) Gabriel se détend / se relaxe en **faisant** du yoga tous les matins / chaque matin.
b) Julie s'entraîne toutes les semaines / chaque semaine en **écoutant** de la musique.
c) Nous nous parlons en **nous promenant** / en **marchant** dans le parc.
d) En **mangeant** des repas équilibrés, Sandrine restera en bonne santé.

Q3 I have never been on a diet. In my opinion, you must eat a balanced diet. My parents and I eat a lot of vegetables. However, I often snack between meals. I know it's bad for your health, so I've decided that I will give up sweets completely.

Q4 Je ne mange que / Je mange seulement de la nourriture saine et je fais beaucoup d'exercice. En ce moment, je m'entraîne pour le marathon de Paris, que je ferai au printemps. J'ai commencé à courir / faire du jogging tous les jours / chaque jour. Maintenant j'ai plus d'énergie, je dors mieux et je suis rarement malade. Je continuerai à courir / faire du jogging dans le futur / à l'avenir.

Page 44 — Unhealthy Living

Q1 a) In my opinion, alcohol is the most dangerous drug.
b) la plus dégoûtante — I don't smoke any more, because tobacco has the most disgusting smell.
c) la plus difficile — Natalie believes stopping smoking is the most difficult thing.
d) les plus nocifs — Undoubtedly, (addiction to) smoking and drugs are the most harmful.

Q2 a) Si elle buvait de l'alcool, Camille se sentirait malade.
b) Je me sentirais mieux si je mangeais plus de fruits et de légumes.
c) Tu pourrais / Vous pourriez devenir accro(s) si tu prenais / vous preniez des médicaments fréquemment.
d) Si Hassan se droguait, je ne voudrais plus être son ami(e) / copain / sa copine.

Q3 serait; n'habitait pas; beaucoup moins chère; aime manger seulement

Q4 My best friend has started smoking / to smoke cannabis. That worries me because cannabis can cause mental health problems. (Personally) I would never try it because it's too harmful. What should I do? I would like to tell someone that he smokes / is smoking it, but I don't want to lose a friend.

Page 45 — Illnesses

Q1 a) J'ai trop mangé, alors / donc j'ai mal au ventre / à l'estomac.
b) Si tu bois / vous buvez trop de boissons sucrées, Nina, tu auras / vous aurez mal aux dents.
c) Ils ont mal à la gorge depuis une semaine.
d) Delphine a mal aux pieds à cause de ses nouvelles chaussures.

Q2 a) Coralie s'est cassé le bras lorsqu' / quand elle était plus jeune.
b) Je me suis fait mal au pied — Je me suis fait mal au pied en jouant au foot(ball).
c) ils / elles se sont cassé le(s) jambe(s) — Ils / Elles se sont cassé le(s) jambe(s) devant l'hôpital.
d) Hugo s'est fait mal — Hugo s'est fait mal au dos lorsqu' / quand il a eu un accident.

Q3 a) Thomas: I can't stop coughing. This morning I was out of breath / breathless and I felt weak.
Doctor: It's probably / undoubtedly just a cold. Take this (cough) syrup every evening before sleeping and you will soon feel better.
b) Caroline: I don't feel well. I have a fever and I have been sick three times today.
Doctor: It seems to me that you have the flu. You should stay in bed until you don't feel ill any more.

Q4 Mon frère s'est fait mal en faisant du vélo. Nous sommes allés à l'hôpital en voiture. Son bras était très rouge et il nous a dit que la douleur était insupportable. Le médecin a vu son bras et il a dit que mon frère se l'était cassé. Quand nous sommes rentrés chez nous, il est allé au lit / s'est couché immédiatement.

Pages 46-47 — Environmental Problems

Q1 a) There **will be** more and more rubbish in the sea in the future.
b) Our area **will become** dirtier if we leave rubbish everywhere.
c) The world **will be** too polluted, if we / people continue to use plastic bags.
d) Businesses **will have** to use less packaging on their products.

Q2 a) Les catastrophes naturelles comme les tremblements de terre sont terribles.
b) Le changement climatique a causé des inondations dans certaines régions.
c) Il y a souvent des feux de forêt dans les pays chauds.
d) Les sécheresses ont rarement lieu dans ce pays.

Q3 a) Carole had understood the disadvantages of nuclear energy.
b) avaient produit — Frédéric and Amélie had produced too much rubbish at home / too much household waste.
c) avait averti(e) — Henri had warned me about the dangers of climate change.
d) avais trié — I had sorted out the recycling before the meeting.

Q4 a) on
b) assez
c) devoir
À mon avis, on ne fait pas assez pour arrêter le réchauffement de la Terre. L'un des problèmes les plus graves / sérieux est le déboisement. On détruit des fôrets chaque année. On devrait les protéger, mais le problème est compliqué.

Q5 a) The water quality of the river has become better recently.

Answers

b) les pires — Our town / city has the worst levels of air pollution in the region.

c) la meilleure — Forests are the best thing to make the air cleaner.

d) pire — The problem of oil in the sea is getting worse.

Q6 Je suis très fâché(e) / en colère à cause des ordures / déchets dans notre quartier. Nous habitions dans un beau village avec beaucoup d'espaces verts, mais maintenant notre environnement est endommagé. Bientôt il sera trop tard. On doit / Il faut changer notre comportement et s'occuper de la campagne.

Q7 a) Alain: De nouveaux genres d'énergie seront la seule solution au réchauffement de la Terre.
b) Fleur: L'énergie renouvelable ne pourra pas produire assez d'électricité.
c) Alex: On utilisait beaucoup de charbon pour créer de l'électricité, mais c'était mauvais pour l'environnement.
d) Ida: Il y a trop de pollution dans l'air. On devrait arrêter de brûler le pétrole.

Q8 My family and I make a big effort to protect the environment. My parents (have) sold their car and they walk to work. If there were cycle lanes in my town / city, my parents would go everywhere by bike. We believe that it's important to reduce (the) carbon dioxide in the atmosphere.

Page 48 — Problems in Society

Q1 You should have ticked a), d) and e).
a) La pauvreté est un problème très grave / sérieux dans la société.
b) Il y a beaucoup de chômage dans ma ville.
c) Il n'y a pas assez d'eau potable.
d) Le harcèlement a lieu dans les écoles et au travail.
e) Il me semble que le problème du racisme devient pire.

Q2 a) Il est possible de faire plus pour protéger les droits de l'homme.
b) Il est nécessaire de — Il est nécessaire d'avoir plus d'HLM.
c) Il est important de — Il est important d'aider les gens qui sont déprimés.
d) Il faut — Il faut créer de nouveaux emplois / métiers dans cette ville.

Q3 a) (The) inequality between the richest people and the most disadvantaged people is a global concern.
b) I love living in a diverse area. That's why I'm in support of immigration, because I like getting to know other cultures.
c) There are lots of refugees in the world who have had to leave their country because of war.

Q4 My town / city was / used to be very industrial in the past, but since the big factory closed (down), there are few / aren't many jobs. The high levels of unemployment have caused an increase in the number of homeless people who live / are living on the streets. We must create more businesses before the situation gets worse.

Page 49 — Contributing to Society

Q1 a) Claude brings his rubbish to the recycling centre each week.
b) Aurélie, bains, eau — Aurélie doesn't have baths any more because that wastes water.
c) sacs en papier, sacs en plastique, environnement — I use paper bags, because plastic bags damage the environment.
d) viande, réchauffement de la Terre — I don't eat meat because that contributes to global warming.

Q2 a) Demain, Jules chantera avec sa chorale **pour collecter** des fonds.
b) Georges fait des campagnes **pour combattre** la pauvreté.
c) Mon lycée donne de l'argent chaque année **pour aider** des associations caritatives / organisations charitables.
d) Ma sœur était bénévole en Afrique. Elle y est allée **pour construire** une école / un collège.

Q3 a) it is
b) allé
c) Il faut que
In my opinion, it's very important to engage yourself politically. Last week, I went with my parents to the town / city centre where there was a demonstration / protest to support the rights of refugees. The government must do something to help them.

Q4 Je veux faire quelque chose pour aider la société, alors / donc bientôt je deviendrai bénévole pour une association caritative / organisation charitable qui a pour but de nettoyer notre quartier. Je passerai deux heures par semaine dans la forêt à ramasser les ordures / déchets. J'aimerais le faire plus souvent, mais je n'ai pas assez de temps en ce moment.

Page 50 — Global Events

Q1 a) Have you already been to the World Cup?
b) toujours — My brother always used to watch / watched football matches.
c) encore — The Edinburgh Festival has not started yet.
d) encore / toujours — Camille is still watching / still watches the Olympic Games.

Q2 a) La course a eu lieu à Londres en avril.
b) être — Ils / Elles sont allé(e)s à Wimbledon le mois dernier parce qu'ils / elles adorent le tennis.
c) être — Nous sommes arrivé(e)s en retard / trop tard, alors / donc nous n'avons pas pu regarder le tournoi d'athlétisme.
d) avoir — Cette année, un Anglais a gagné le Tour de France.

Q3 a) Sabine: Daniel, have you already / ever been to a music festival?
Daniel: Of course. I'm a fan of metal (music), so I went to a festival last year. I met lots of interesting people.
b) Sabine: In three months, I hope to go to Barcelona where there will be a big pop concert. You would be silly not to come with me.

Answers

Daniel: It doesn't mean anything to me / I don't fancy that. That event will be a waste of time.

Q4 Les événements internationaux sont très importants parce qu'ils aident à créer de bons rapports entre les pays. Aujourd'hui, j'ai vu une affiche pour un concert de jazz américain dans ma ville en juillet. D'habitude / Normalement, je n'écoute pas du jazz, mais je vais aller à ce festival. J'espère y trouver des amis américains. *Or* J'espère trouver des amis américains là-bas.

Pages 51-53 — Mixed Practice

Q1 Kévin: Le nombre de SDF / sans-abri dans ce pays est un grand problème et il est devenu pire récemment.
Rania: Oui. La pauvreté a augmenté à cause du mauvais état de l'économie. Qu'est-ce que nous pourrions faire / Que pourrions-nous faire pour aider?
Kévin: Je suis bénévole pour une association caritative / organisation charitable qui distribue de la nourriture gratuite. Nous avons besoin de plus d'aide dans la cuisine. Tu pourrais / Vous pourriez nous aider, si tu voulais / vous vouliez.
Rania: J'adorerais vous aider.

Q2 a) Yesterday, I ate too many sweets and that made me vomit / sick.
b) I used to hate / hated sport. To stay fit / in shape, I used to walk / walked instead of driving.
c) Some diets that are in fashion at the moment are bad for your health.
d) People say that / It is said that eating more fruit and vegetables can prevent certain illnesses.

Q3 I moved to a big town / city a month ago, but I can't bear all the noise. I can't get to sleep when I go to bed in the evening because of the traffic. The pollution also worries me because I often have difficulty breathing. I believe that I am going to become ill.

Q4 a) Il y a sept ans, il y a eu un grave tremblement de terre au Japon. Plus de cent pays et associations caritatives / organisations charitables ont aidé les victimes.
b) La semaine prochaine, il y aura une manifestation internationale contre la guerre. Beaucoup de gens croient que le gouvernement devrait essayer d'empêcher la violence entre les pays.
c) Ma sœur travaillait pour une association caritative / organisation charitable. Elle aidait les gens dans les pays pauvres qui avaient dû quitter leurs maisons après un ouragan. Elle leur a donné de la nourriture, de l'eau et des vêtements propres.

Q5 Nature is my passion. When I finish my studies, I will look for a job at / with a charity which protects the environment. I am disgusted when I see images on the TV of sea birds covered in oil. If I could do something to improve the situation, I would feel happier.

Q6 En 2015, mon amie / ma copine Inès et moi sommes allé(e)s à Londres pour regarder le rugby. C'était une rencontre sportive mondiale qui a rassemblé des gens de tous les coins du monde. Nous avions fait un bon voyage à l'avion, mais quand / lorsque nous sommes arrivé(e)s à Londres, l'air était très pollué. C'était vraiment désagréable.

Q7 a) Do you drink alcohol before sleeping / going to sleep? According to (the) evidence, if you drink less of it in the evening, you will sleep better.
b) Have you tried to stop smoking in the past? Did you fail because of a lack of help? Ask your doctor for advice.
c) If you eat too much saturated fat, you will increase the risk of a heart attack. If you are not sure how to eat a balanced diet, read this information.

Q8 Il y a une campagne pour sensibiliser le public aux bandes dans ce quartier. Les agents de police / Les policiers avertissent / préviennent qu'elles pourraient être très dangereuses. Il y a quelques jours, des filles ont harcelé une vieille femme et puis elles ont volé son argent. La police serait reconnaissante de votre aide. Prenez soin / Occupez-vous de vos voisins et restez vigilants.

Q9 a) Angela: If I was / were the mayor, I would install more water fountains (in order) to give homeless people better access to drinking water.
b) Marine: I would organise a music festival, because there aren't enough activities for young people. It would also be good for the local economy.
c) Nawal: In my opinion, this town / city needs more cycle lanes because we must reduce traffic. Air pollution is dangerous for those who live here.

Q10 My brother used to be / was a drug addict. He used to take drugs and get drunk every day. *Or* He took drugs and got drunk every day. Because of his addiction, he got a lot thinner. All of my family used to think / thought that he would need long-term care. However, now he is much better. He no longer takes drugs and he has a new job.

Q11 a) J'utilisais beaucoup d'eau. Je laissais le robinet ouvert quand je me brossais les dents. Après avoir participé à une campagne récente, je sais maintenant comment économiser l'eau.
b) Dennis a toujours cru que le recyclage est important. Il dit que c'est notre responsabilité d'aider la planète en recyclant tout ce qu'on peut.
c) Je trouve souvent beaucoup de déchets / d'ordures dans le parc. C'est dégoûtant quand les gens les jettent partout! Je mets toujours mes déchets / ordures dans la poubelle. On devrait respecter la nature et garder propre le parc.

Q12 Le WWF est une association caritative / organisation charitable qui travaille avec les gouvernements pour protéger les animaux qui sont en danger. En 2007, l'association / l'organisation a commencé un événement qui s'appelle Earth Hour, qui a eu lieu le dernier samedi de mars. Le but était de combattre le changement climatique en demandant aux gens d'éteindre leurs lumières et de ne pas utiliser d'électricité pendant une heure.

Answers

Section 6 — Travel and Tourism

Page 54 — Where to Go

Q1
a) Joaquim and I would like to go / travel to Spain.
b) aux — Our grandparents are going to America / the USA this year.
c) en — This winter, I'm going to spend the holidays in China.
d) en — Are you going to go to Scotland next weekend?
e) au — My brother wants to visit them in Wales.

Q2
a) Evan et ses amis / copains vont en Angleterre en été.
b) Ellie va en France avec son copain / son petit ami, mais je vais en Belgique.
c) Mes cousin(e)s et moi sommes allé(e)s à la campagne ensemble.
d) Beaucoup de gens vont en Suisse chaque année.
e) Je vais aller à Londres en novembre.

Q3 Last year, I went to Italy with my family. We spent five days in Rome and then a week at the seaside / by the sea. It was the best holiday of my life! However, this year we're not going abroad, because it's too expensive.

Q4 J'adore l'Afrique! J'ai visité douze pays africains et c'est un beau continent. Le Maroc est mon pays préféré / favori parce que les gens / habitants sont très sympa / gentils et aimables / sympathiques. Le mois prochain j'irai en Tunisie, où on peut nager / se baigner dans la Méditerranée.

Page 55 — Accommodation

Q1
a) Je vais chercher un petit hôtel.
b) to sleep — Mon père préfère dormir dans une tente.
c) going — Lucie aime faire du camping.
d) stay — Nous pouvons loger / rester dans une auberge de jeunesse.

Q2
a) You can't relax at a holiday camp / summer camp. There are too many people and (there is) too much noise.
b) I stayed in / at a luxury hotel, but my (bed)room was dirty.
c) There is a hole in my tent. When it rains / When it's raining, it rains (on the) inside too!

Q3
a) Bed and breakfasts are more expensive than campsites.
b) less comfortable than — The campsite was less comfortable than the hotel.
c) as clean as — The dormitories are as clean as the family room.
d) as much as — The caravan will not cost as much as the holiday cottage.

Q4
a) **Guillaume:** Où logeras-tu / resteras-tu en Espagne?
Nannette: Je logerai / resterai dans une auberge de jeunesse au bord de la mer.
b) **Guillaume:** J'adore les auberges de jeunesse parce qu'on peut rencontrer beaucoup de gens intéressants.
Nannette: Je voulais aller dans une / en colonie de vacances, mais c'était complet. Cependant / Pourtant, l'auberge de jeunesse est très bon marché, donc j'ai économisé de l'argent.

Q5 Everyone should go camping this summer. There are lots of good campsites in France offering / which offer lots of services / facilities including washing machines and electricity for the caravans. Who wouldn't like to spend a week in the open air, free to do what they want?

Page 56 — Getting Ready

Q1
a) Let's visit the travel agency / travel agent's.
b) Choisissez — Choose your accommodation.
c) Donnez — Give me your identification / proof of identity / ID.
d) Réserve — Book / reserve a (bed)room with a balcony.
e) N'oublions pas — Let's not forget our sunglasses.
f) Faites — Pack your suitcases now!

Q2
a) Où sont tes / vos bagages, Sam?
b) Quand vas-tu / allez-vous en vacances avec tes / vos parents?
c) Combien de billets as-tu / avez-vous besoin d'acheter, Josie?
d) Pourquoi a-t-elle trois maillots de bain?
e) Comment met-on / mets-tu / mettez-vous cette crème solaire?

Q3
a) Clara would like to book / reserve a room from the 25th of March to the 2nd of April.
b) préférerais — A single bed is too small. I would prefer a double bed.
c) aimeriez — You would like to book / reserve a (bed)room that overlooks the square.
d) serait — We think that it would be better to stay in the town / city centre.
e) voudraient — My grandparents would like a (bed)room with air conditioning.

Q4 Je voudrais réserver une chambre avec deux lits superposés du vingt-neuf juin au quatre juillet. Nous arriverons vers / à environ vingt-deux heures. L'année dernière, nous sommes resté(e)s dans une chambre qui donnait sur la mer. Serait-il / Est-ce qu'il serait possible de rester de nouveau / encore dans la même chambre?

Page 57 — Getting There

Q1
a) J'y vais en voiture.
b) Katy y est allée en moto.
c) Il y a deux aéroports à Paris.
d) On ne peut pas y aller à pied.

Q2
a) I have never travelled by plane because it scares me.
b) revenus — Hamid and Tom returned / came back from Algeria by boat.
c) duré — The coach journey took / lasted several hours.
d) montée — Two hours later, Anna got on / boarded the train.
e) attendu — At the (train) station, we waited (for) 40 minutes.

Answers

Q3 a) **Suzie:** J'aime voyager en train. Le train pour Londres n'est jamais en retard.
Ed: C'est vrai, mais je le trouve trop cher. Je dois prendre l'autobus / le bus.
b) **Alice:** J'ai acheté un (billet) aller-retour, mais mon train est parti en avance.
Olive: Je suis désolée, madame. Nous vous rembourserons le prix de votre billet.
c) **Ajay:** Je pense que les voitures sont plus fiables que les trains.
Paul: Tu as tort! / Vous avez tort! Les voitures vont trop lentement et il y a toujours beaucoup d'embouteillages sur les autoroutes.

Q4 My journey to Montreal was very comfortable. I got on / boarded the plane at ten o'clock in the morning, and I got off it seven hours later. When I landed, it was midday in Canada. After having got off the plane, I went to the hotel by bus. I'm already looking forward to taking the return flight.

Pages 58-59 — What to Do

Q1 a) Il y a quelques belles plages à Nice.
b) Nous pouvons faire de la voile cet(te) après-midi.
c) Je veux louer un parasol aujourd'hui.
d) Ces glaces sont délicieuses.
e) La mer est plus chaude qu'hier.
f) Beaucoup de gens aiment se (faire) bronzer.

Q2 a) Yesterday evening, it rained a lot in Lyon.
b) We liked the zoo a lot.
c) He / She liked the visit to the theme park.
d) When it rained, we went to the bookshop.

Q3 a) My step-mother was visiting / used to visit / visited the tourist attractions in Monaco.
b) allait — Who was going / used to go / went to the playground with the children?
c) nageaient — Mélanie and Chloé were swimming / used to swim / swam in the outdoor swimming pool.
d) faisais — When I was small, I used to go / went skiing in the mountains.
e) Visitiez — Did you (used to) visit the Louvre (museum) when you were living / lived in Paris?

Q4 a) Le premier jour, visitez l'office de tourisme et demandez une carte / un plan de ville.
b) Après avoir trouvé la cathédrale, marchez jusqu'à la rivière / jusqu'au fleuve.
c) Faites une visite guidée pour découvrir des choses à faire.
d) Choisissez une carte postale d'un bâtiment célèbre.

Q5 a) What is there to do here?
b) loin — He travelled far to find the castle.
c) sur — The old cathedral is (located) on the square.
d) au-dessus de — I believe the tourist office is above the post office.

Q6 a) J'ai essayé de parler en français **pendant que** j'étais en vacances à Paris.
b) Ils / Elles ont trouvé un bon restaurant **dès qu'**ils / elles sont arrivé(e)s.
c) Nous irons au marché **même s'**il fait mauvais.
d) **Puisque** le musée est fermé, nous allons au centre commercial.

Q7 a) la nouvelle station balnéaire
b) proper future
c) team games
This summer, come to spend a week at the new seaside resort for young people. Situated on the Mediterranean Coast, the resort will offer you the opportunity to try several water sports and (to) participate in team games. You will also be able to perfect a hobby, or learn something new.

Q8 Je viens d'aller à Bruxelles et cette ville m'a beaucoup plu. Mon frère et moi avons fait une visite guidée et le lendemain nous avons visité des musées. Le village miniature était étonnant / incroyable et il y avait aussi de beaux jardins / un beau parc. Le soir on pouvait marcher / se promener à travers le centre-ville. Nous retournerons / reviendrons à Bruxelles l'année prochaine.

Page 60 — Practical Stuff

Q1 a) Mia (has) missed her train.
b) There is an error on the bill.
c) The shower doesn't work / isn't working.
d) It's a shame that the bed linen isn't clean.
e) The car broke down / has broken down.
f) The repair is expensive / costs a lot.

Q2 a) Il n'y avait personne à la réception / à l'accueil.
b) Malheureusement, il n'y a plus de vélos à louer.
c) Je n'ai trouvé ni le bloc sanitaire, ni les toilettes.
d) Le / La réceptionniste ne fait rien pour nous aider.
e) Il y a une heure d'attente parce qu' / car il n'y a que deux serveurs.

Q3 a) My suitcase has been stolen / was stolen by a man.
b) present passive — The tourists are helped by a police officer.
c) imperfect passive — They were (being) attacked by a bird on the beach.
d) proper future passive — Passports will be checked at passport control.
e) perfect passive — The luggage has been left at the bus / coach station.

Q4 J'étais à Toulouse depuis trois jours quand ma moto est tombée en panne. Quel désastre! Je suis allé(e) à un garage près de la chambre d'hôte, mais les réparations ont coûté assez cher. Demain je vais aller à Montpellier. Cette fois, il n'y aura plus de problèmes!

Pages 61-63 — Mixed Practice

Q1 a) J'aime faire de la planche à voile, alors / donc je veux réserver un logement qui est près de la plage.
b) Il est resté dans une station balnéaire où il pouvait se (faire) bronzer à côté de la piscine pendant toute la journée.
c) La cathédrale était en face de notre hôtel, alors / donc nous avons fait une visite guidée quand nous sommes arrivé(e)s.

Answers

    d) Je voulais aller au parc d'attractions, mais c'était trop loin du camping.
    e) L'employé(e) à l'auberge de jeunesse a loué des VTT / vélos tout terrain pour nous.

Q2 **a)** I went to China and I visited all the main tourist attractions.
    b) As he's a fan of water sports, he will go to the Mediterranean coast.
    c) Next year, we will go on a boat tour of the Channel Islands.
    d) This year, I went to Carcassonne, where I visited the church near (to) the city centre.
    e) When I go to Germany, I really like walking / going for a walk in the countryside.
    f) I hope that the weather is nice when she goes to Italy. She wants to see the volcano in Naples.

Q3 **Julianna:** Est-ce que tu t'es bien amusé à l'hôtel de glace, Stephan?
    Stephan: C'était fantastique! Il faisait très froid, mais j'avais mis beaucoup de vêtements dans ma valise.
    Julianna: Je suis très jalouse de toi. Les photos de ton séjour sont belles.
    Stephan: Il y avait quelques désavantages / inconvénients. L'hôtel est toujours complet, donc j'ai dû réserver ma chambre en avance. Le trajet à l'hôtel a pris beaucoup de temps / a duré longtemps aussi.

Q4 I am the manager of a hotel on the edge of a lake. In the past, it was very old-fashioned. Now, it's more modern and it has become very popular with tourists. This year, the hotel will be open from the 1st of February to the 31st of August. All bookings / reservations made before the 1st of June will include a free trip / outing to the neighbouring church.

Q5 **a)** Je voyagerai à Grenoble pour regarder le Tour de France, alors / donc je voudrais réserver une chambre avec (une) vue sur la route nationale.
    b) Ils / Elles ont organisé une randonnée pour le premier jour de leurs vacances. Ils / Elles ont besoin de prendre des sacs de couchage parce qu'ils / elles feront du camping dans les montagnes.
    c) On peut réserver un séjour organisé à l'agence de voyage. Nous avons choisi un séjour qui offre une visite du musée et deux chambres dans un hôtel célèbre.

Q6 We are going to travel on / by foot from this village (here) to that mountain (there). Tomorrow, the temperature will be more than thirty degrees, so I have bought you lots of sun cream. Put it on frequently, please. You should all have a tent and a rucksack / backpack so that you can easily carry all your things.

Q7 **a)** Mon père n'a jamais aimé aller en vacances dans les pays chauds. Il déteste utiliser la climatisation dans les chambres d'hôtel.
    b) Elle adore visiter New York, mais elle préfère loger / rester dans un logement où il n'y a pas de bruit.
    c) Nous restions toujours dans un camping au pays de Galles. Je n'aimais pas partager les toilettes / WC et les douches avec d'autres gens / personnes, alors / donc maintenant nous logeons / restons dans une chambre d'hôte.

Q8 **Omaira:** Do you have the timetable for the metro / underground? I think we (have) missed the last train. What are we going to do?
    Yvonne: Don't worry, we can get / take a taxi to the hotel.
    Omaira: I would like that because my suitcase was damaged at the airport.
    Yvonne: What a journey! If there hadn't been a four-hour delay at the airport, we would have arrived a lot earlier!

Q9 **a)** This winter, we will go to Finland. We will fly to Helsinki and then we will hire a car (in order) to go to the bed and breakfast in Tampere.
    b) Last year, she went to Belgium. Planes scare her / She's scared of planes, so she decided to take the ferry. The journey took / lasted more than twelve hours.
    c) This afternoon, I'm going to France. I'm worried about being late, so I want to arrive at the (train) station at least one hour before the departure time.

Q10 Il fait très chaud ici en Australie. Nous avons passé beaucoup de temps près de la mer où c'est plus agréable. Hier, Diana a fait du ski nautique. Malheureusement, elle est tombée et elle a dû aller à l'hôpital. Je vais visiter un des lacs roses demain. Je t'enverrai quelques photos!

Q11 **a)** Yesterday, I got lost during the tour. I was taking photos of the buildings when everyone left without me!
    b) He forgot to validate his ticket on the tram, so he had to get off at the next stop. Next time, he will not make the same mistake!
    c) My mother asked a police officer for help because I had put my passport in my handbag which had been stolen.

Q12 Mon amie / Ma copine adore visiter le Brésil. Il y a deux ans, elle a passé trois semaines dans un camping au milieu de la jungle. La seule manière d'y aller était de voyager sur une route très étroite, puis de prendre un bateau sur la rivière / le fleuve. À l'avenir / Dans le futur, elle préférerait loger / rester dans une auberge de jeunesse.

Section 7 — Current & Future Study and Employment

Pages 64-65 — School Life

Q1 **a)** L'informatique est une matière utile pour les jeunes.
    b) Est-ce que tu aimes / vous aimez l'allemand? *Or* Aimes-tu / Aimez-vous l'allemand?
    c) Il trouve que les math(ématique)s sont difficiles.
    d) Elle préfère la musique, mais elle n'est pas très douée.
    e) Ma sœur déteste le dessin.

Answers

f) Pourquoi est-ce que la physique est trop compliquée? *Or* Pourquoi la physique est-elle trop compliquée?

Q2 a) On the first day back at school, lessons will start at eight-thirty / half past eight.
b) We have humanities / history-geography twice a week.
c) The biology lesson lasts for an hour and a quarter / an hour and fifteen minutes.
d) The break is too late in the day.
e) The headteacher made a new timetable last year.

Q3 a) Elle peut utiliser les ordinateurs pendant sa pause-déjeuner.
b) voulons — Nous voulons des vacances plus longues en été.
c) peuvent — Ils / Elles peuvent prendre des cours d'EPS au terrain de sport.
d) veux — Je veux avoir des salles de classe (qui sont) bien équipées.

Q4 former / old school; bully me; listen to them; to take an exam

Q5 a) My mother thought that private school was better.
b) conditional — I would prefer to have less homework and less reading.
c) proper future — You / We will have to repeat / resit the year if you / we get bad marks. It's unfair!
d) imperfect — You used to put me / were putting me / put me under too much pressure during my exams!

Q6 a) Il faut laisser votre portable chez vous.
b) Il ne faut pas parler dans la bibliothèque.
c) Il faut porter une cravate, et il ne faut pas se maquiller.
d) Il faut lever la main pour parler.
e) Il ne faut pas courir dans les couloirs.
f) Il ne faut pas entrer dans les salles de classes pendant la récré(ation) / la pause.

Q7 My timetable is going to change in year 11. I will have more modern languages and I will start algebra. I am scared / afraid that it is / will be too complicated for me, because I find numbers difficult to understand. Like you, I am interested in Chinese, but the teacher is quite strict. He has already given detentions to me.

Q8 J'étudie dans un internat depuis quatre ans. Mes parents me manquent, mais mes amis / copains sont devenus ma famille. Les professeurs étaient très compréhensifs quand / lorsque j'ai échoué (à) un examen, et le directeur / directrice / proviseur dit qu'il donnera le résultat à mes parents à la fin du trimestre.

Page 66 — School Events

Q1 a) Un billet pour le spectacle de fin d'année coûtera cinq euros.
b) Il y a une rencontre parents-professeurs la veille de la mi-trimestre.
c) Samedi il y aura une vente de charité au gymnase.
d) Le groupe théâtral jouera sa pièce cette semaine.

Q2 a) They used to use / were using / used it during sports day.
b) le — He's going to visit it during the school trip.
c) le — Our school chess team will win it!
d) les — She cancelled them because the journeys would be dangerous.

Q3 a) **Cosette:** J'ai adoré l'échange espagnol.
Antoine: Moi aussi! J'ai beaucoup aimé ma correspondante et sa famille.
Cosette: Ce que j'ai aimé le plus était l'excursion au stade de foot(ball).
b) **Antoine:** Je n'y suis pas allé parce que mes parents ne m'avaient pas autorisé.
Cosette: Tu peux y aller la prochaine fois. Nous reviendrons / retournerons en Espagne l'année prochaine.

Q4 (The) parents' evening took place last week. After having discussed my school report, I thought that my parents would be in a bad mood because I break the rules from time to time. However, the teacher told them that I am going to move up to the next class and that pleased them / made them happy.

Page 67 — Education Post-16

Q1 a) Which subjects do you intend to study?
b) ont l'ambition d' — They have an ambition / They aspire to study chemistry, but it's really difficult.
c) a besoin de — Théo needs to find a job.
d) n'ai pas envie de — I don't want / have the desire to continue my studies, because I would prefer to work straight away.

Q2 a) Nous irons à l'école militaire en septembre.
b) arrêteront — Ils / Elles arrêteront l'école à la fin de la seconde.
c) seras — Tu seras apprenti(e) dans l'entreprise de ton père.
d) réussirai — En terminale, je réussirai (à) tous mes examens.
e) prendra — Après son bac(calauréat), il prendra une année sabbatique.

Q3 a) **Marcus:** What's the closest university? I would like to study there.
Georgia: There is one (of them) in town. You could / would be able to save money if you lived at home.
b) **Mikhail:** I'm fed up of school. I won't go to university.
Dafydd: It isn't for everyone, but your apprenticeship will be educational too.
c) **Bethany:** I've always wanted to start my own business after school.
Sheldon: That's an ambitious idea! You must work without pay / for free at the beginning.

Q4 Je voudrais étudier à l'université / à la faculté mais si le niveau est trop difficile, je ne me débrouillerai pas. Le conseiller d'orientation m'a dit qu'il faut être travailleur et intelligent, ce qui m'inquiète. Cependant, mon père adorait vraiment l'université / la faculté. J'ai besoin de prendre bientôt une décision.

Answers

Page 68 — Languages for the Future

Q1 a) He would like to learn Welsh.
b) My father is bilingual.
c) If I had the time, I would learn another European language.
d) I find the Russian alphabet very difficult.
e) You have to practise languages frequently.
f) Languages change / are changing all the time, so / therefore you never stop learning them.

Q2 a) Les langues étrangères me permettent de communiquer plus clairement.
b) plus facilement — On peut voyager à travers le monde plus facilement.
c) plus rapidement / plus vite — J'apprends d'autres langues plus rapidement / plus vite.
d) plus fréquemment — Je pourrai travailler à l'étranger plus fréquemment.
e) plus franchement — Fred parle plus franchement lorsqu'il est / quand il est en vacances.

Q3 a) I think that it's a waste of time to learn foreign languages since everyone speaks English. In my opinion, we don't need them.
b) My parents learnt Latin at school, but nobody / no one uses it to communicate! Today, languages like Chinese and Spanish are much more useful.
c) In the future, I would like to be a civil servant abroad, therefore / so for me modern languages are the most important subjects.

Q4 J'ai commencé à apprendre l'allemand et l'espagnol il y a quatre ans, mais je devrai laisser tomber une langue l'année prochaine. Je préfère l'espagnol. Si je le parlais couramment, j'aurais un meilleur salaire / une meilleure paie et de meilleures possibilités d'avancement. En apprenant plus de langues quand je serai plus âgé(e), j'aurai plus de choix dans ma carrière.

Page 69 — Applying for Jobs

Q1 a) Qui as-tu / avez-vous rencontré à l'entretien?
b) Que devrais-je écrire sur ce formulaire / cette fiche?
c) Qui travaille bien en équipe?
d) Qui n'a pas d'expérience?
e) Que sais-tu / savez-vous de notre entreprise?
f) Que dois-je faire pour poser ma candidature?

Q2 a) I have just received a response.
b) viens de poser — You have just applied for this job / position.
c) vient d'envoyer — Gabrielle has just sent her application letter.
d) venait de voir — Sam had just seen the advertisement for his ideal job.
e) venaient de finir / terminer — They had just finished school.

Q3 J'ai lu une annonce sur votre site web. Je voudrais poser ma candidature au poste de secrétaire dans votre société / entreprise. Le mois dernier j'ai terminé un stage (en entreprise) dans un bureau, qui m'a donné l'expérience nécessaire. Je pourrais commencer immédiatement / tout de suite.

Q4 a) **Émile:** In your opinion, what qualities must you have for this job / position?
Michel: You must be warm and (self-)confident. I have all the skills that you need.
b) **Émile:** And why have you applied for this job / position?
Michel: I would like to have a job that is more exciting than mine.
c) **Émile:** How long have you worked in / been working in this industry?
Michel: For ten years. I did (some) work experience here years ago and I learnt a lot.

Page 70 — Career Choices and Ambitions

Q1 a) Je voudrais être interprète parce qu'on peut gagner beaucoup d'argent et habiter à l'étranger.
b) Ma meilleure amie / copine va devenir artiste. Elle aimait le dessin à l'école, alors / donc maintenant elle suit son rêve.
c) Je veux être mécanicien(ne) parce que j'aime les voitures. À l'avenir / Dans le futur, je travaillerai pour une marque célèbre.

Q2 a) During her childhood, Sophie used to want / wanted to become an engineer.
b) a quitté — Last week, my mother quit(ted) her job.
c) était — When he was twenty (years old), my grandfather was a builder / mason.
d) a travaillé — Vincent worked as a police officer for five years.

Q3 a) comme serveuse
b) il n'y a pas beaucoup de *Or* il y a peu de
c) reflexive
J'ai un petit job / un travail à temps partiel / un travail à mi-temps depuis l'année dernière. Je travaille comme serveuse dans un restaurant le samedi. Ce n'est pas passionnant, mais il n'y a pas beaucoup de / il y a peu de débouchés dans cette ville et je m'entends bien avec mon gérant / ma gérante.

Q4 I have always dreamed of becoming a journalist, because it's a very rewarding / enriching job and I would be able to travel. However, I don't know if this career would be practical. Sometimes it is difficult to find jobs in journalism and I would prefer to work as soon as I complete my A-Level(s).

Pages 71-73 — Mixed Practice

Q1 a) Après son bac(calauréat), Flora passera deux mois à l'étranger pour améliorer son français.
b) S'il a / S'il obtient de bonnes notes, il étudiera la médecine parce qu'il voudrait être infirmier.
c) Je pourrais avoir un petit job / un emploi à temps partiel / un emploi à mi-temps pendant que j'étudie, pour obtenir / avoir plus d'expérience.
d) Ella veut prendre une année sabbatique. Elle a travaillé dur pendant ses examens, alors / donc elle devrait se détendre / se relaxer.
e) Mes parents pensent que je devrais faire des études supérieures, mais (moi,) je veux être apprenti(e) plombier / plombière.

Answers

Q2 L'art dramatique est ma matière préférée / favorite parce que les cours sont vraiment intéressants. D'habitude / Normalement, il est interdit de parler fort en classe, mais pendant les cours d'art dramatique on peut / nous pouvons faire beaucoup de bruit. J'étudierai l'art dramatique au lycée. Je crois que je suis très doué(e), alors / donc je voudrais devenir un acteur / une actrice célèbre.

Q3 **Loïc:** Can you introduce yourself?
Marc: Of course. My name is Marc and I'm very interested in sales.
Loïc: I see on your CV that you have little / don't have much professional experience.
Marc: That's true, but I did (some) work experience in a shopping centre a year ago.
Loïc: Could you / Would you be able to study for a degree at the same time as working?
Marc: Absolutely. I used to study two evenings a week in my former / old job.

Q4 The King Graham School / Sixth Form College will present itself to the public next Wednesday. Come to see our modern buildings and our big sports ground during our open day. We have the best results in the country. Start your ideal career with us, where you would get / obtain the marks that you've always dreamed of / of which you've always dreamed!

Q5 Au début de l'année, j'ai eu un mauvais bulletin scolaire. Cependant / Pourtant, après l'échange scolaire, j'ai amélioré ma note en français parce que mon correspondant / ma correspondante et moi avions parlé en français pendant toute la semaine. Pouvoir parler aux étrangers est une compétence de grande valeur, alors / donc j'étais très content(e).

Q6 **Julia:** In my career, I would like to set an example (for others) to follow. I hope to become someone famous, like a singer or a model. I could never be a teacher.
Yanic: Me neither. You would have too much homework to mark / correct and too many lessons to teach. However, my ideal career would be different to yours. I would do voluntary work.
Julia: Will you need to study to do it?
Yanic: No. I think that experience will count (for) more than qualifications.

Q7 a) Normalement / D'habitude je suis les règles (scolaires), mais il y a quelques élèves dans mon collège / école qui harcèlent les autres. À l'université, les étudiants se comporteront mieux.
b) Puisque j'habite loin du collège / de l'école, je me lève à six heures et demie / six heures trente le matin. Maintenant, je me réveille toujours tôt, ce qui pourrait être utile pour le travail.
c) J'allais à une école publique. L'enseignement était très bon et le conseiller d'orientation m'a aidé(e) à trouver un apprentissage.

Q8 Yesterday I started my part-time job as a lifeguard at the swimming pool. I am saving money / putting money aside to pay for my studies in the United States. I used to earn / was earning money by baby-sitting for my teachers, but I wanted to have a more regular job. I intend / plan to leave in two years.

Q9 a) **Luc:** Je ne veux pas aller à l'université ou travailler à l'intérieur. Que devrais-je faire? / Qu'est-ce que je devrais faire?
Henri: Si vous aimez être en plein air, vous pourriez faire un apprentissage en jardinage.
b) **Layla:** Mes meilleures matières sont les math(ématique)s et la physique. Je les ai toujours comprises.
Henri: Vous pourriez devenir ingénieur. Vous devrez étudier la chimie aussi.
c) **Henri:** Il est important de choisir une carrière que vous aimez / qu'on aime. Qu'est-ce que vous voulez faire à l'avenir / dans le futur?
Zoé: J'aime la musique et mon professeur dit que je suis assez douée, mais le manque d'emplois m'inquiète / je m'inquiète du manque d'emplois.

Q10 My father is a computer scientist / IT technician. My mother didn't use to work, but she has just started a new job in a shop. They want me to go to university because they never had the opportunity to get / obtain a degree themselves. I feel obliged to do it.

Q11 a) We are looking for someone to do the washing-up in our restaurant. You have to be hard-working and punctual. The interviews will take place next week.
b) Would you like a part-time job after school? We / They (are in) need (of) assistance / help at the public library. The salary is fair and you can take breaks.
c) The job / position of secretary in our office will be available (starting) from January. The ideal candidate would have at least two years of experience and an A-Level qualification.

Q12 Il y a deux jours, j'ai eu une retenue parce que je m'étais endormi(e) pendant mon cours de chimie. Je suis toujours fatigué(e) en ce moment parce que je prends des cours supplémentaires le soir pour étudier la mode. Si j'échoue (à) mes examens, je devrai redoubler et je ne pourrai pas suivre mon projet pour l'année prochaine.